Pineapple Promise
สัญญาสับปะรด

A Thailand Adoption Memoir

HOLLY STOFA

DECRYPT COACHING
PEAK PERFORMANCE IS AN INSIDE JOB

MARYLAND

This is a true story.

Some details have been changed without altering the overall content. All opinions and assertions are those of the author and not intended to represent the opinions or recollections of other people, herein mentioned or not.

Some names have been excluded completely. Others have been changed, including all names of Thai people, Thai orphanages, and any children other than our own, to shield their identity and protect the privacy of the staff members, other friends, and the children.

All personal, anecdotal use of actual given American names of adults is done with the express permission of the people mentioned. Nicknames, references, or titles without names are used in some instances and the publicly available mention of a well-known person in another.

All statements of fact, opinion, or analysis expressed are those of the author and do not reflect the official positions or views of the U.S. Government. Nothing in the contents should be construed as asserting or implying U.S. Government authentication of information or endorsement of the author's views.

Cover Design: Holly Stofa.

Cover image of a Thai street market is courtesy of Canva.com. All free photos, music, and video files on Canva can be used for free for commercial and noncommercial use.

Print ISBN: 978-1-66787-996-3
Ebook ISBN: 978-1-66787-997-0

To Jessi,

We would do it all again.

Love, Mom

And for those still waiting...

Contents

Acknowledgements

Thank you to the people that have helped me bring this project to life.

My husband, Vince, for supporting me throughout this entire journey, from the very first discussion of adoption, all the way through writing this book, which was never part of the plan.

Our three children, and my mom, who have entertained and considered my questions at weird times, seemingly out of the blue, about what they remember regarding parts of the past decade plus.

My amazing colleagues and friends, who are the best editors I could ask for, because they are consummate professionals and care about me, and willing to hold me accountable. I knew I could count on them to make this project better without losing my authenticity of voice.

The people mentioned by name in this book who agreed to allow me to express fully, publicly what they mean to our family and our adoption journey.

All those who were not specifically named for various reasons, for everything you've done, for me and my family.

Each of you taking the time to read this story. You are continuing to breathe life into the work and the messages it shares.

Preface

The original project idea was to document for our daughter the story behind us adopting her. I wanted to put down, in one place, all the things that aren't interesting to a young child, tween, or teen, but might be later, before I forgot details. It took on an additional dimension in becoming a resource for educating others and increasing awareness about the complexities of adoption. And finally, it became a healing journey for me, to work through the trauma I experienced while my daughter was going through her own. Ultimately, it is a compelling testimony on the power of faith, hope, love, and determination.

Revisiting some of the very hard times was exhausting and incredible. I was able to process things that I simply couldn't while we were going through them and just trying to get through one day at a time. The initial version of this project was handwritten in a notebook, pen to paper, allowing me to form new connections in my mind. In the early mornings, I would get up and devote time to write, one piece of the story at a time. I'd make notes of other topics for another session. Step by step. Many mornings, and sometimes evenings, after writing, I would sit and cry, and grieve, and heal. New pathways emerged of cognitive understanding of what we lived, that have helped me to love and appreciate my daughter, my sons, and my husband, even more, and with greater empathy.

With this book, like the adoption process, I just kept figuratively putting one foot in front of the other. This project has given me the gift of peace about our adoption process. It has allowed me to share with others the impact they had on our family and in our lives. While intended as a gift for our daughter, the giving has magnified in every direction. It serves as a reminder to always tell people how I feel, and how they have influenced me and made an impression. In doing so, they are inspired to pass it on. Kindness, connection, and love. The gifts that keep giving.

Why *Pineapple Promise*? The phrase captures and symbolizes the connection within our family. It's interesting and insightful to view life through a connection lens, such as considering what people in different parts of the world are doing and things that are happening at the same time. Concurrent paths of seemingly disparate people and events that ultimately come together. This thread of connection is present throughout the book.

People have come together over food for as long as stories have been told. We all need it; most of us enjoy it; and it sustains us throughout life. I've always loved pineapple. The combination of sweet and sour, each pineapple having its own taste, unique to the stage of ripeness at which it's consumed. Like people, a pineapple develops and evolves, balancing the parts of itself, while its core remains intact. Although pineapple is not indigenous to Southeast Asia, three of the top 10 pineapple producing countries are within the region, including Thailand. Whatever processes these Southeast Asian countries have used to cultivate the fruit, we found it to be among the best we'd ever had.

As it turned out, pineapple was our daughter's favorite fruit. It was a common part of meals at her first home and one of many tastes of Thailand she loved, too. Such a simple commonality and shared joy later served as a tie that was already formed before we were joined as a family. And the promise? We made it early; to 'her' and to our family, as it was, and as *we* would become. We stuck to it, even when times were hard, and we always will.

Pineapple Promise
สัญญาสับปะรด

Introduction

When you decide to adopt a child, and then actually do it, you're asked a lot of questions. None of the questions have the short, simple answers, people seem to want. Especially in today's world of brief attention spans and catchy headlines, there is a tendency not to go below surface level on a single subject. But adoption is a deep subject, no matter how you approach it; a wholly human endeavor that cannot be adequately captured in brief or reduced to a headline without ignoring some of the spectrum of emotions therein.

From the outside looking in, many people take an altruistic view of adoption and think of it as 'saving' someone, an act done primarily for the child. For me, I personally identified with the child I sought, having experienced the loss of a parent early in life, and I viewed adoption as an opportunity to love someone in the spaces where they didn't feel loved. I hoped that same warmth would fill those spaces in me, too. I didn't realize this until I explored my own reasons for wanting to adopt.

Whatever people think about adoption, they are generally not shy to tell you, whether you ask their opinion or not. In some ways, it's like being pregnant and choosing a baby name. If you tell someone the name(s) you're considering, they will often, without hesitation, share their thoughts. However, once the baby is born and you announce the name, it is then attached to a human being right in front of them and their opinions are usually reserved. Similarly, no one asks in front of our daughter why we chose to adopt. Looking at her in front of them, it makes sense.

Adoption is complex and multi-faceted. Every adoption story is unique, from the reasons a person or couple choose to adopt, to the details of the human story of the adopted child or children. If you ask 100 adoptive families about their experiences, you will hear 100 different stories. Every human is an individual, so each story about a group of individuals coming together, through adoption or otherwise, is specific to that group. Certainly, though, there would be recurring themes and some similarities. Determination, trauma, and love, not the least of these.

In looking back over our family's journey to and through the adoption process, I am struck by two things that I have attempted to capture in this work: The amount of struggle, from first becoming a family with biological children, to growing our family through adoption; and the number of people who supported us, in ways large and small, in the U.S. and in Thailand, many not realizing the impact they had. Some of them are mentioned by name in this book, with their permission, to publicly express our gratitude for their empathy, support, and love. It got us through many years of preparation, process, and transition. Many other people are not mentioned specifically or by name, or their names have been changed, to protect their privacy, both American and Thai. To everyone who has walked a portion of this journey with us, we thank you, with our whole hearts. Please know every kind word, gesture, or act of assistance is deeply appreciated and will never be forgotten.

Before we had biological children, my husband, Vince, and I discussed adoption. The idea had always been with me, and I was curious how he felt about it. My assumption had been that the topic was more straightforward for women, although, it turns out men adopt more often than women. To my delight, Vince was open to it, at least in theory. We agreed, however, that we wanted to try to have biological children before considering adoption, although not necessarily *instead* of adopting. In the following years, we had our two amazing biological sons, Boston, and Quinn, each of whom came with their own struggle in entering the world.

In moving on toward adoption, over a 10-year period, faith and determination, and the support and assistance of others, enabled Vince and I to stay the course. I continued to believe there was a tiny person on the other end of all the process and took every step along the way to get to that little girl. Whenever Vince needed to hear it, I reminded him that 'she' was out there, and we just had to keep going unless something made it clear we should stop. All the while we were raising our two biological sons, who were the saving grace for everyone when it came time to finally meet our daughter, Jessi.

People often envision a happy unification in adoption while ours was anything but that. You take a lot of training courses and do your own research, but nothing truly prepares you for the real thing. There is so much grief and loss in adoption and everyone processes grief in their own way. When you add a language barrier and individual personalities, there is simply no algorithm to determine how an adoption transition will go. Ours was painful and beautiful and worth every minute. We made it through to the other side.

In laying out our journey, certainly some details are lost, and dates are difficult to recall. I have used emails, paperwork, photos, and conversations with my family to help me piece together the facts, as best I can. The important parts, though, are mental and emotional rather than chronological, and they are captured here. This book gives the necessary attention to articulate what we lived, as an example of what an adoptive child and family can go through. It cannot be summarized in a five-minute conversation.

The original primary purpose in sharing our story was to document for our daughter what led us to her, which begins with why we were motivated to adopt, and how and who we were as a family before her adoption. In revisiting our history, our story demonstrates the depths of the human capacity to love, and the ability to achieve difficult things when you remember your 'why,' consistently taking one step at a time.

Resilience rings loud and clear from our daughter's story. Our family's adoption story. Thank you for taking the time to share in our journey. In reading it, may you feel compelled to examine what really matters to you, moved to support others whenever you can, and inspired to do hard things.

Part One

CHAPTER 1

Why Adoption?

When people learn I am an adoptive mother, they ask one question more than any other. It is sometimes phrased as "What made you want to adopt?" The essence of it is always, "Why?" My inner voice and intuition have always answered without hesitation, "Why not?" I heard the question often enough that I started trying to understand the genesis of the question, since it was never something I considered. In attempting to get to the root of the question, I challenged myself to honestly answer it, regardless of its impetus. What was my motivation for wanting to adopt?

As far back as I can recall, adoption of a child seemed like something I might do; a calling I heard from deep inside. As I pondered the topic, I identified with the abandonment I presumed orphans must feel. My parents were high school sweethearts and married very young. My mom became pregnant shortly after they were married, and they split not long after I was born. It was just my mom and me for several years. I didn't know any different and it took years before I understood the concept of a 'dad' by seeing other families. While I saw my father off and on until I was about seven years old, we did not have an established relationship and I never called him "Dad". That was just too uncomfortable. But I understood he was my father.

When I was a young adult, a friend's father told me a story that I didn't recall from my childhood. He and my mother were also friends. One day while the four of us were spending time together, my friend spoke to his father and began a sentence with "Hey, Dad…" I apparently turned to my mother and asked, "What's a dad?" My friend's father said the event stayed with him his entire life in terms of illustrating the importance of being a present father. When he and his wife later divorced, he committed to making sure his younger daughter never had to ask that question of her mother.

As fate would have it, I had close friends, now lifelong friends, that also grew up without their fathers for much of their lives. Despite different stories, the net result was a group of friends amongst whom not having a dad around was normal. I didn't think much about the absence of a dad since I had never known the presence. Another friend, whose house I visited periodically, had both parents in the home. I remember being fascinated by her father, watching her parents interact with each other, and seeing him care for my friend the way a 'dad' does.

While I was curious, I never felt I was missing anything. Nonetheless, my subconscious mind and inner child's heart felt the loss. I think it was the void in me that fueled both my desire to try to take that away from someone else and my belief that I could fill that hole with love, for them and for me. When a parent leaves, it makes it hard to trust people. It is really about trusting them not to leave. This played out more as I got older than as a child. When I was a kid, I simply wanted to be accepted, like all kids. I was always willing to put myself out there with friends and later when dating. At times, this was to my own detriment as I allowed myself to be treated less than respectfully because I didn't want people to leave my life. The fear of abandonment runs deep. I went back and forth between latching onto people I barely knew and intentionally choosing people who were not emotionally or otherwise available. I avoided true connection with those who were.

When I met my husband, Vince, something about him engendered my trust, instantly, that he would not leave me. I remember thinking that I could put my heart in a box, give it to him for safekeeping, and that he would guard it with his life. It was comfort and security I had never known, and it drew me to him. Interestingly, he and my father have birthdays only two days apart and some similarities including being large in stature and embodying a balance of seriousness and silliness. Perhaps I had subconsciously picked up on that, having had visits with my father over the years. The difference was I felt I could count on my husband to stay. Consequently, I believed that, if *I* could learn to trust, certainly Vince and I, together, could help someone else to do the same.

In growing up with my mom and without my father, both her presence and his absence factored into my development, my belief systems, and the filter through which I viewed life. Of course, they still do. I'm just more aware of it now. My father is a good man, and I don't harbor resentment for the choices either of my parents made when they were so young – before or after ending their marriage. As I grew through various stages of life, I sometimes considered my parents at the same age, and what their life scenario had been at that time. The older I got, the more I could cognitively understand their different perspectives. Nonetheless, the trauma of losing a parent, for any reason, remains. You can heal from it. You can understand the circumstances and reasons behind it, but you can never erase the pain that you felt, even if subconsciously at the time, and the scars left behind. While I don't dwell on it, a deeper awareness enables me to empathize with others on the topic, at any stage of their journey.

From the time I was in middle school, if not sooner, I have always instinctively considered other people's feelings. Despite being shy and sensitive, my internal flame often allowed me to push past my fears both for myself and in defense of others. My natural inclination as a defender grew into a desire to provide opportunities whenever possible. There is so much to be said for opportunity. People born into adverse circumstances or who face significant challenges generally don't want people to feel sorry for them. They want equal opportunities, and they often want things more deeply than those to whom much is given or provided early in life. To dismiss someone based on their background is to underestimate the power and drive of the human spirit and the infinite potential therein. There is no progress in feeling sorry for someone. To make a difference is to act on what you feel. To provide opportunity and encouragement. To believe in someone and do something about it, even if you have never met them. Their humanity makes them worthy of love, belonging, and opportunity. I often say, "You do *what* you can, *when* you can." I wanted to do what I could to make a difference for someone else, who might not otherwise be able to bring their fight to life.

Simply put, adoption is hard, every part of it. From the concept to the paperwork, to waiting, to dealing with transition trauma, and forming a connection, which I struggled with. There are a million reasons to allow your fears to take hold and question whether to begin and then, whether to continue. Every time those feelings arose for me or for Vince, I would ask "If we are not equipped to do this, to push through, then who is?" And we would press on.

People often think of adoption as a Christian thing to do, probably because Christians adopt at a higher rate than non-Christians. While Vince and I are Christian, it is not the sole reason we chose to pursue adoption. There are over two billion Christians worldwide which means, depending which estimates are considered, they outnumber orphans approximately 13 to one globally, and are about one to one in the United States. If you factor in all the kind and loving people with other belief systems, and equally capable of being parents, it certainly compounds the possibility of dramatically reducing the global orphan population, on paper. However, there are many reasons why people, regardless of their belief system, may or may not choose to adopt a child, not the least of which is socioeconomic status, particularly in countries outside of the U.S. As a first-world, wealthy nation, by global standards, the U.S. accounts for almost half of all adoptions worldwide out of the more than 100 countries that are part of the Hague Adoption Convention.

"The Hague Convention on Protection of Children and Co-operation in Respect of Intercountry Adoption (Hague Adoption Convention) is an international treaty that provides important safeguards to protect the best interests of children, birth parents, and adoptive parents in intercountry adoptions." The full list of countries is available on the U.S. Citizen and Immigration Services website. https://www.uscis.gov/adoption/ immigration-through-adoption/hague-process (at the time of printing).

All to say, there are plenty of people who *technically* could adopt, but don't. It may not cross their minds, may not be something in which they're interested, or they may have other responsibilities, such as eldercare, which preclude taking responsibility for an additional person. They may admire it in others, but have no desire to do it, like how I feel about those who run marathons. It's inspiring *and*, with my knees, it's not for me. In terms of adoption, I knew we couldn't do everything for everyone, but we could do something for someone. As with many things in life, it's the start that stops most people. When we began the process, we had no idea how we would pay for the adoption process, but I never doubted that we would figure it out. We understood our 'why,' and I knew we would find a way.

Another issue mentioned by people who were curious was the idea that "you don't know what you're going to get." At first blush, it is as if people think their own genes are somehow superior to others. Certainly, some people do believe this, whether they are consciously processing their words as such or not. On the other hand, people generally feel more comfortable with familiarity. That's part of human nature. However, even when people have biological children, we also do not "know what we're going to get." We know the two sets of DNA going into the child, but we do not know what traits, conditions, or gene mutations will appear when the child is born and throughout their life.

There are other examples of people deeply loving other living beings with whom they do not share DNA, such as their pets. People, obviously, do not give birth to their pets, but they certainly care for them as family members and grieve the loss of one as though they were human. We've all heard people refer to their pets as 'fur babies'. Additionally, anyone who has coached kids and wholeheartedly cared for them also knows the depth of feeling one can have for children who are not biologically theirs. Most of us can imagine giving such a child a home and family if they needed it.

For anyone who questions whether a person can truly love a child that does not have their blood, you absolutely can. I have and I do. The human capacity to love is amazing. Still, if this question features prominently in one's mind, it is possible that adoption is not a good fit for a particular family or for the prospective adoptive child.

CHAPTER 2

Starting Our Family

Vince and I began our marriage in Braintree, Massachusetts, a suburb located south of the city of Boston. As a United States Secret Service (USSS) couple, we knew that our time in the Boston area was limited. We were intent on enjoying it and not immediately trying to have children. If you've visited Boston, you might not think of it as a warm place in terms of weather or people. We loved the culture of the cold, New England sports mecca, and had a loving and welcoming group of friends. We had been introduced to them and brought into the circle by one of Vince's colleagues, who had become a close friend. New Englanders tend to be "all set" with friends by the time they're adults, so we considered ourselves fortunate to be part of a close-knit group of wicked good people from the next town over, Quincy (pronounced 'Quinn-zee').

Our first Christmas in Boston, Vince and I were alone at our small duplex rental, with no family in the area and no money or annual leave available to travel home to Maryland. On Christmas Eve, we attended a service that had a warmer than average feel for a Catholic church. Being early in our marriage, we were still working out our preferences in terms of practicing religion. I was raised in the United Methodist church and Vince was raised in the Catholic church. My maternal grandfather had been a minister and Vince's family was a devout practicing Catholic family. As a couple, Vince and I opted to focus on our shared Christian beliefs and faith as our anchor. Over the years, we have attended many churches of various faiths, keeping our eyes and hearts fixed on what is most important and on sameness rather than on differences.

On that first Christmas evening in Massachusetts, a small group of our closest friends showed up on our snowy doorstep to celebrate with us, having drinks and playing games. It is one of my most cherished memories because we felt so seen and loved. Over the next few years, we made many more special memories with our Boston native friends.

Two years into living in Massachusetts, we decided to begin trying to get pregnant. Interestingly, Vince remembers it being more difficult than I do. Perhaps, in the grand scheme of life including adoption, looking back, it seems simple. While it's somewhat blurry to me, I believe there was a new lingerie wardrobe intended to spark the mood whenever the monthly timing was right. It made perfect sense to me as a woman thinking the male lizard brain was that basic, but for Vince it applied pressure to what is never meant to be a stressful situation. Shortly after July 4th, during which I enjoyed a couple of alcoholic drinks, we learned I was already pregnant. I eased my mind by doing some basic research and assured myself it would all be fine.

The pregnancy itself was uneventful in the best possible way as I was healthy throughout. I had the chance to take in two history-making Red Sox games in the 2004 season that ended the 86-year drought of World Series Championships for Boston baseball. Along with my field hockey coaching colleague, I attended Game 4 of the American League Championship Series (ALCS) between the Red Sox and the New York Yankees. Big Papi hit a game-ending walk-off homerun, over five hours into the game, in the 12th inning. Making it through this game without going to the restroom for fear of missing something monumental was quite the feat for a pregnant woman. After the greatest comeback in sports history, with the Red Sox winning the next three games and ultimately becoming American League Champions, Vince and I had the unexpected opportunity to see Game 1 of the World Series between the Red Sox and the St. Louis Cardinals, while sitting atop the infamous Green Monster.

One day after the Boston Red Sox swept the St. Louis Cardinals to win the 2004 World Series, I went into Massachusetts General Hospital (MGH) for a sonogram to learn the gender of our baby. I asked that the technician write it down and put it in an envelope that I would open later that evening at dinner with Vince. He and I had begun discussing names. I liked the idea of a name which honored the city and team that meant so much to us but did not want to name our baby after a specific player. We talked about the name 'Boston' and ran it by our local friends who all gave their approval and described it as 'wicked awesome' or some version of the same. Vince liked it for either a boy or a girl and I was torn about using it as a girl's name. That evening, in a downtown Boston Irish restaurant, we opened the envelope. The note read, "It's a boy!" Vince and I looked at each other and smiled. I said, "Boston it is!"

Despite being in New England, I often wore tank tops in the dead of winter because baby Boston was like an internal space heater. Two and a half weeks before the full-term due date, I went in for a Friday checkup. As the technician listened for the baby's heartbeat, I couldn't hear it, but figured I was missing something. I saw the look on her face change as she moved the stethoscope around, attempting to find the heartbeat and listening closer. She left the room and returned with a doctor who did the same thing. Shortly thereafter, the doctor explained I would need to be admitted because it was possible the baby was in distress and might have to be delivered very soon. After eight months of a normal pregnancy, tears rolled down my face as panic set in.

I called Vince to update him and tell him where to find my suitcase, prepacked, in the baby's room. I was given an epidural in case they needed to perform an emergency caesarean. Concurrently, I was induced to attempt a vaginal delivery, but did not progress quickly. Boston's heartbeat had stabilized without any discernible reason for what had caused the prior erratic and low heartbeat. As the snow fell outside my hospital window, Friday night became Saturday, and then Saturday night, with little progress. I had shifted around in my bed over the course of 24 hours, trying to get comfortable, and eventually the epidural connection came loose. I went from complete numbness to full labor pains without any gradual build up. In this dramatic, unexpected scenario, I convinced myself the catheter had punctured my bladder because the pain was so excruciating. I demanded it be removed, uncharacteristic of how I communicate with medical professionals or anyone, only to find the pain still present. I asked the nurse, "What *is* that?" Her response was, "Labor pain." My first thought was, "Oh, shit..." The epidural was replaced, and I was given the opportunity to take a nap and calm down. When I woke up, the doctor said, "Are you ready to have a baby?" And I was. With Vince by my side, and one of our close, local friends also in the room, taking photos for us and providing much needed moral support, I began to push. Early Sunday morning, Boston was born, in Boston.

Vince and I adapted to life as new parents, having no idea what we were doing and were relieved whenever grandparents visited. We moved into a slightly larger house in Quincy that overlooked the Boston Harbor for our remaining year in Massachusetts. When Boston was nine months old, I became pregnant with our second child. We had thought 18 to 24 months apart would be a good distance but had opened the possibility given it had not happened immediately with Boston. We learned our babies would be 17 and a half months apart. Some evenings when I was rocking Boston and the baby inside was kicking him in the back, I questioned the timing, but trusted it would work out as it should.

Vince had been trying to get an assignment back in Washington, D.C. for over a year. Vince traveled back to the D.C. area to attempt USSS Counterassault Team (CAT) training, a grueling six-week course with a low pass rate due to its difficulty and requisite, uncompromising standards. While the President's Protective Detail (PPD) covers and removes the 'protectee', the term used to describe the principal whom USSS is charged to protect, CAT enters to neutralize the threat. There is no room for error. Mid-course, Vince sustained a significant muscular injury that might have derailed many, but he managed to complete the training. He had felt additional pressure for the family to get back to the D.C. area and to a support network, and it pushed him through the pain. Vince doesn't talk much about this ordeal, but a close colleague of his recounted for me the inspiration that Vince provided with his performance. Having successfully made it to CAT, we opted to move while I was still pregnant, with only one baby to manage.

Having considered moving to the Virginia suburbs of D.C. to be near many of my girlfriends, we decided instead to move to Maryland to be near Vince's parents. We knew he would be away much of the time, and they were the ones I'd most likely call if I needed help. On our house hunting trip, during a hot July in Maryland, I squeezed myself into compression tights due to vein issues during pregnancy, and we visited 45 homes in three days. We selected one of the first we had visited as our favorite. After closing on the house, we needed to have some work done before moving in. Meanwhile, we stayed nearby at Vince's parents' house and both of us were working full-time. One morning, as I rushed to get some laundry done before heading to the office, I slipped on the basement stairs and fell directly onto my tailbone. Vince was still home and, with Boston in tow, came to find me on the stairs screaming in pain. I was taken to the hospital just about a mile away by ambulance and admitted to the labor and delivery unit, once again, in case the baby needed to be delivered quickly.

Fortunately, the baby was assessed to be fine, surrounded by much cushion to protect him. I went home and was basically on bedrest for the remainder of the pregnancy. My tailbone had become my primary source of discomfort and pain. Based on Boston's delivery, during which he had difficulty moving through the birth canal and had suffered some initial nerve damage, and the fact that any pushing would put pressure on my fractured tailbone, it was determined that I would have a C-section this time around. In the meantime, we moved back into our prior home. I remained uncomfortable as my tailbone was going to take a long time to heal. Less than one month later, we welcomed Quinn to the family, his name in honor of our second home in Massachusetts, and the group of friends that were our family in Boston.

CHAPTER 3

Pursuing Domestic Adoption & Other Options

Each week, during the local evening news, there was a segment called Wednesday's Child, which was a spotlight feature on a child who was awaiting adoption in the Washington, D.C. area. While pregnant with Quinn, there was a segment on a beautiful little girl named Stephanie. She had caramel colored skin, large inquisitive eyes, and black hair that was styled into ringlet curls. Everything in me wanted to go get this child and love her but the thought, during pregnancy, was overwhelming. Additionally, many foster care and adoption programs do not allow you to adopt a child while pregnant for the understandable reason that each child deserves and needs the care of their parents during transition to a new life. Vince and I agreed that, even if allowed, it was too much for us at that time. I prayed for Stephanie and let go of the idea of her joining our family as the big sister.

Two years later, Stephanie was still on my heart and mind. The boys were then two, and three and a half years old, which meant Stephanie was about seven years old. I could not shake my curiosity about her and was moved, again, to try to find her. I searched through the old Wednesday's Child clips on the news website. I called the number provided and learned Stephanie was "still in the system," meaning, she had not yet been adopted. I told Vince we needed to go get this child. I had heard informally that the prospects for white families adopting black children in Washington, D.C. were not good; most children in the D.C. adoption system were black and approximately 85% of kids in D.C. were adopted by their foster families. Vince and I had discussed and decided against fostering. Even if we could get our heads around potentially having a child come into our home and then leave, we were not willing to intentionally have the boys experience such loss so early in life, while not yet old enough to truly understand. Vince was most opposed to the potential of fostering and the subsequent heartbreak, not only for the kids, but for himself. I understood and supported this decision we made together.

In hopes of demonstrating our sincerity of intent and capacity to love, we enrolled in the required adoption certification training in D.C., rather than in Maryland, since Stephanie was in D.C.'s foster care system. There were approximately 10 to 12 people in our training course, including many potential foster parents, as prospective foster and adoptive parents were all required to receive the same training. Without foster families, many children would languish in unhealthy situations. There was one other white person in the group. We didn't assume this to mean our chances were better than in the past, but noted it, nonetheless, in that we were not the only white parents following our hearts in this way, in this space, despite whatever odds may or may not have been working for or against us.

Presumably, all the people in this room were there out of love for kids and a desire to help. The cost of adding a child to one's family is, of course, significant. With the cost of a D.C. suburb mortgage, public sector salaries, and two toddlers in child-care, we had very little extra monthly income. Yet, we were privileged to feel confident we had the necessary means to add another child to our family without having to focus on whether we would receive the compensation generally provided to support foster parents in assuming the additional expenses. Our confidence was rooted in faith that we could make a way.

During this time, we moved our younger son from what had been the nursery into a larger bedroom with his big brother. Our thought process was that they would shortly become accustomed to sharing the room and, by the time their sister joined the family, they would not associate her arrival with any loss of something for themselves. They were children, after all, and still very much focused on their own needs.

As expected with the new assignment, Vince was on near constant travel. Then-Senator Barack Obama was running for President of the United States for the first time. I was more concerned than usual, thinking Obama's race would prompt racists with weapons to come out of the woodwork, increasing the threat level, ultimately more so to USSS agents than to Obama himself. Sure enough, during one trip, while Vince was away, he called to say a colleague would be coming by to get his extra gear. I knew this meant threats had increased, just as I had suspected. Still, even with the heavy travel rotation, Vince was able to attend almost all the training sessions. On the final night of class and certification, we learned Stephanie was being adopted by her then foster family. It was the best match she'd had to date. Two conflicting truths were simultaneously true: I was elated for her *and* heartbroken for us.

Through this failed adoption experience, I grieved a child I had loved without ever having met her. It didn't matter that she wasn't born of my body, my feelings for her were real. This child, who had stayed in my head and heart for over three years at this point, was a catalyst in our lives. I wondered if I would recognize her if I ever saw her out in public. I thought about how relatively close she had come to being part of our family and how she never knew that. I prayed that her new family made her feel seen and loved the way we had hoped to do. I let go the visions of her being a big sister and having the opportunity to just be a kid in our family. I recognized the gravity of her existence in our lives, even as we were going through it, and I allowed myself grace in processing the loss before considering next steps.

We stayed in the D.C. system, since we had, in fact, been certified as prospective adoptive parents. We attended events including one on my birthday. I remember feeling so hopeful and excited at the prospect of finding our match. Many of the attendees were seeking to adopt their first child and most wanted a baby or a toddler. The presentation focused heavily on the fostering and adoption of teens, a critical need for which not every family is suited. We were concerned about bringing in a significantly older child and potentially exposing our toddlers to trauma-driven behavior which might negatively impact them. As a child of multiple traumas (which are not all addressed in this work), I was unwilling, as was my husband, to take on this risk.

Four months later, our adoption certification in the D.C. system expired. I cried as I stared at it hanging on the kitchen wall where it had been since we received it. I felt another door closing in our quest to grow our family through adoption. I cried again for Stephanie, the beautiful brown girl with black curls who had begun preparing our hearts for adoption. Roughly one year later, on the other side of the world, another brown-skinned girl with black curls would be conceived and, unbeknownst to us, was destined to become part of our family.

We began to question whether adoption was for us. Although it had been a calling in my heart for as long as I could remember, it started to feel like it wasn't in the cards for us. Prior to marriage, I had always envisioned myself with three children and was not ready to let go of this dream. While I was not one who relished being pregnant and despite the difficulties with each of the prior pregnancies, still, I was willing to consider it one more time. Vince and I agreed that pregnancy past 39 years of age was not in my best interest. Each family makes their own choices, and this was ours. There was still time.

Vince had always really wanted a girl. With each of our two pregnancies, prior to learning the gender, he said, "I think it's a girl," and possibly even repeated it after we had been told otherwise. He had previously been an elementary physical education teacher and enjoyed seeing his female students achieve as much as boys. I had, thus far, loved being a boy mom, perhaps based on assisting with caring for my two younger brothers into my teenage years. It was familiar territory. We heard about an intrauterine insemination (IUI) process in which the chances of one gender or another could be increased, although not guaranteed. Our understanding was that the sperm was spun to generate some separation based on gender given the different characteristics of male and female sperm. The process was estimated to increase the chances from 50% to 70% for a specific gender. While the inability to guarantee 100% success may have made some people uncomfortable, it was this statistic that made us comfortable with the process. In our minds and hearts, it preserved space for God to make the ultimate determination whether we became pregnant this way at all and, if so, whether the child would be a boy or a girl. Given the cost of the process, and that we already had two beautiful, healthy children, we agreed to attempt only one cycle.

Vince and I each had responsibilities in the process. I visited the medical office several times for hormone level measurements and injections. Vince, of course, had to provide the sperm. To say he did not enjoy the process would be an understatement. The day came for insemination. I don't recall whether Vince was in town, but I went alone given it was a straightforward procedure and closer to my work than his. If you envision a turkey baster, your imagination is close to accurate. After the procedure, the doctor and staff left the sterile room and I laid still on the table, hips up, alone. I had not anticipated feeling any emotions and was surprised when I was overcome by the feeling that I was not alone, a sense that a divine presence was in the room with me. I gave thanks for the opportunity and prayed that, if it was meant for us to become pregnant in this way, and have a daughter, that He would make it so. I felt odd physical sensations inside, as I lay still, and was convinced God was at work forming our next child. In the coming weeks, we waited for the news and were disheartened to learn we had not become pregnant after all. Vince's immediate response was "Well, then, I guess we're meant to adopt a daughter."

Had we become pregnant with a third child through this process, we almost certainly would not have further pursued adoption. I still believe God was in the room, but that He was there to ensure space was preserved in our lives for our future daughter, already born on the other side of the world.

When we first saw Stephanie, Boston was just over a year old, and I was pregnant with Quinn. At that time, Stephanie was five years old. Had we been able to adopt her then, the boys would have been so young that they would eventually only remember life with a big sister already present. Even when we pursued the adoption of Stephanie, years later, the boys were three and four years old and Stephanie seven. We still felt comfortable with bringing in a big sister, particularly one who had expressed a maternal instinct. It seemed to us that, while she may have sought to nurture her brothers the way she dreamed mothers did, as she had commented in a video, we would have been doing the same for her. Given the gender difference, the issue of birth order had not deterred us from trying to adopt Stephanie.

Now that Stephanie had been adopted by her then foster family and IUI had not resulted in pregnancy, we were back to considering adoption options. Knowing that adoption was bound to take time, more time, we decided we should shift to a younger child. Boston had developed quite the personality and we felt he deserved to retain his place as the eldest sibling. Quinn would then be relegated to the dreaded middle child slot, only slightly better than being the youngest in some estimations, including his own, if you ask him now. And so it was, our perspective changed, and our adoption quest began, again.

CHAPTER 4

Choosing International Adoption

In seeking to adopt, we weren't specifically hoping for a newborn or infant. In fact, we actively did *not* want that. We had gotten past the point of lugging around extensive baby gear everywhere we went, were well beyond diapers, and were getting a full night's sleep. Beyond these somewhat trivial matters in considering adopting a child, we knew that many couples were seeking to build a family with a child for the first time and many desperately wanted babies. Combined with the fact that we had already been blessed with two children, these were all good reasons to consider an 'older' child. Additionally, older children are usually harder to place. Any child over four years old, and sometimes as young as three, is considered 'older' in the world of adoption, which was still younger than the boys.

I spent time exploring various charitable domestic adoption websites, still discouraged by the thought of trying again to work through the local foster care system. In looking at private adoption websites, there were countless beautiful, loving couples, telling their stories, and making the case to a prospective birth mother to choose them to give her baby a family and an opportunity for a good life. It became clear that neither domestic option, public or private, was the path for us and I began researching international options.

The People's Republic of China and the Republic of Korea (also known as South Korea) quickly stood out as countries with established adoption programs. Each had a system that, while efficient in process, was neither quick nor inexpensive. It was difficult to justify spending so much money to adopt a third child when we had not even started college savings for our other two children. Living in the Washington Metropolitan Area was expensive. With two children in full-time childcare, we hardly had any expendable income and, without both of us working, we would not have been able to make ends meet.

I came upon Guatemala as an international adoption option I had not previously heard about. The program had a shorter timeline, was less expensive, and the country was in the same hemisphere, all of which I viewed as positives. Meanwhile, here was another population of children in need of loving families. I was excited about the possibility and talked with Vince. Almost as quickly as I felt we had found our program, our hopes were dashed. There was an international scandal regarding Guatemala adoption programs being shut down for fraudulent practices. It was asserted that Guatemalan children had been taken from loving Guatemalan families and put up for adoption for profit against the families' will, and that some had been adopted internationally by unwitting adoptive families. My heart broke for these children and their birth and adoptive families and again, for us, as another adoption door had closed.

We had decided to pursue an overseas posting for our jobs. The likeliest location had become Southeast Asia. Looking at adoption programs in the region, I was able to find enough references to Thailand adoption online to know it was possible but occurred at a much lower rate than the more established programs in other countries I'd researched. On average, Americans adopt over 2,000 children per year from China and 50 or fewer from Thailand. Undeterred, and lacking information that might have made me question the chances of successfully adopting from Thailand – other than lower numbers which I presumed were based on China's well-established programs – we decided Thailand adoption made the most sense. We would be in Southeast Asia for two to three years and have an opportunity to live and learn about the countries, the people, and the many cultures firsthand.

In researching Thai adoption, I stumbled upon information that I would much later learn was related to domestic Thai adoptions, which I understood to require you to live in Southeast Asia for six months before beginning the adoption application process. For an international adoption, we could have begun the process while still in the United States with the assistance of a U.S. adoption agency but didn't know it. So, absent this knowledge, it gave us a break from what had already been a four-year effort to *start* the adoption process. I felt some relief to have a general plan, waiting until we moved to Southeast Asia, always in prayer and attempting to see the signs along the path.

In this same timeframe, our future daughter was born on the other side of the world. It is interesting to consider that this period of peace regarding adoption coincided with her arrival on earth and allowed me to focus on what was a stressful professional period. I knew a year in advance that I had been selected for an assignment in Southeast Asia. In preparation for the assignment, I was entitled to full-time foreign language training. However, because I had taken a counterterrorism assignment, I was unable to participate in full-time language training. Having always felt I had an ability to learn languages, but only ever having studied Spanish in high school, I was motivated to give a tonal language a try. A tonal language is one where a single word can have multiple meanings depending upon the tone in which it is delivered. While simpler than English in grammatical structure, for example, Thai language has five tones: Rising, falling, high, low, and middle. Using the wrong tone can mean saying "rice" instead of "her", for example, while other mispronunciations could be more consequential.

Because of our adoption plans, I started taking Thai language in the evenings, two to three days per week, following a full workday. My Thai language instructor took a holistic approach to teaching language and incorporated cultural lessons. She graciously took my family to multiple Thai cultural events about town to introduce us to Thai culture. We celebrated Thai New Year, 'Songkran', for our first time at Wat Thai DC, a Thai temple located in Silver Spring, MD. We had no idea how many times we would later attend Wat Thai in preserving our daughter's Thai heritage and contributing to her sense of identity.

I picked up Thai language well for a 'farang' (Westerner), particularly given the part-time instruction and focus. I finished with a basic level of conversational Thai, although not nearly enough to have a substantive conversation with a Thai adult. Nonetheless, my Thai language ability was just about right for communicating with a five-year-old and would come in handy years later. While I couldn't have delivered an official keynote address in Thai, I could assure a young child not to worry because she was loved, and we would take care of her.

Vince and I were both excited and nervous about the upcoming move to Southeast Asia. I knew it was something I needed, and wanted, to do for professional development, personal growth, and credibility, and Vince was fully supportive. It was unclear what would happen with an assignment for him, but he was prepared to honor an agreement we made some years prior – that he would serve on PPD and CAT, and I would later serve abroad. It allowed each of us to honor our commitments and meet the missions for which we had sworn to serve our country.

In the time leading up to this adventure and transition, we were met with varying responses from extended family members. We were perceived by some as putting our family at risk for the sake of my career. I had repeatedly *not* taken assignments that would have propelled my career faster and further, because I put family first. There were later times during our stay in Southeast Asia when news would break of yet another school or public shooting, that I felt safer abroad than in the U.S. Some family members openly offered support in person and, if they doubted or questioned what we were doing, they never let us know or made us feel judged. Others struggled to see what we were giving to our

family through this experience rather than the perspective that
we were taking something. I would later experience their optic
when I sat in the airport waiting to take our daughter out of her
birth country. What we were going to give her did not make the
departure any easier emotionally, for either of us. Perspective is
everything. During this planning time, I was particularly grateful
for Vince's unwavering love and support.

People often fear that which they do not know. Uncertainty
is uncomfortable, yet it is at the edge of our comfort zone that
growth occurs. Together, Vince and I were prepared for this
journey of personal growth and life experience. I was committed to serving my country and grateful for the opportunity, one
that far exceeded any dreams I had growing up as a small-town,
big-hearted girl on the Eastern Shore of Maryland. Many people
are thankful to those who serve their country through federal
government service, but some of us are called to *do* it. I was proud
to answer the call despite being grossly misunderstood by some
who chose different paths in life. To each their own.

Even with struggles and challenges, my family and I have
sacrificed less than so many others, particularly the men and
women who serve in uniform and their families; my colleagues
who have served in hardship posts, some to which I've only traveled briefly or read about; and those who have paid the ultimate price. It has been the honor and privilege of my lifetime
to represent and serve my country, especially in a foreign land
alongside friends. I am who I am, as a person and as a mother,
largely because of the experiences of my career, and the caliber
of my colleagues. They are among the most brilliant and creative
minds on the planet. They are problem-solvers and calculated

risk-takers, courageous and willing to do the needful to have a positive impact on the world; doing so in silence, often bearing the weight of inaccurate criticisms we cannot publicly address. We share a fierce sense of patriotism and desire to do good, and they have challenged me to live up to my own potential.

To my colleagues and friends, you are an inspiration, and I am so humbled to have served with you. Thank you for making me better. I am always, always here for you.

Part Two

CHAPTER 5

Southeast Asia Experience

I t is always hot in Southeast Asia. There is a brief spell in the December timeframe where temperatures may dip into the 80s, but not for long. We moved to a large Southeast Asian city in July and had already acclimated to summer heat at home before doing so. Enroute to our final destination, we had stopped over in Hawaii to visit a dear friend and colleague, who graciously hosted us for a few days. The downtime at the beach, relaxing, was a perfect transition and welcome opportunity to shift gears. A chance to separate from home without immediately touching down in a new country. As we left, though, there was a heaviness that set in for the kids. They remembered what had brought us to Hawaii and where we were going, and how little they knew about what to expect.

Through language training, self-study, and talking with colleagues, we had learned some basic Southeast Asian customs in advance of moving. A widespread Asian custom we picked up was taking off one's shoes when entering a home. While foreign to Americans, it makes a noticeable difference in keeping the house cleaner and we still mostly adhere to this practice in the U.S.

We had chosen the option to live in a mostly expatriate neighborhood of the city, given Vince would not be working, at least initially, we thought. The International School was walking distance from our house. The residents included expatriates from all over the world, many Americans, from members of the diplomatic corps to the U.S. private sector, some wealthy Southeast Asian families, and global representation overall. There were so many American officials from multiple agencies in the region that, in a two-year tour, we didn't come close to meeting them all. There were plenty of Americans with whom to associate along with the opportunity to form friendships within the international community. Our sons became fast friends with a diverse group of children and appreciated the comfort of being with other kids who understood what it was like to be new in class, because they had all been that kid at some point.

Our assigned house was spacious and had four bedrooms. The master bedroom was larger than I had ever seen and certainly more than I ever needed. It was lovely but, from a practical standpoint, meant a lot of extra steps to get to the bathroom, which was also huge and covered in white tile from floor to ceiling. Despite there being multiple bedrooms, the boys decided to share a room, just as they had in the U.S. It provided them some comfort and security in having each other near at night. Because it never gets cold in that part of the world, the construction often isn't particularly solid, in terms of wall or roof thickness, or soundproof. Our first week in the house, in the middle of the night, we experienced a storm with thunderclaps so loud the booms woke me from a sound sleep. I sprung up out of bed and went running to the boys' room, slipping on the shiny wood floors around the corners all the way, like in a cartoon. We had never heard anything like it and the boys were crying as I comforted them. It's amazing what you get used to over time.

Most expatriate families employ a helper to assist with household duties and cooking, and sometimes as a nanny. Because Vince would not be working, we had considered forgoing this arrangement, but learned that doing so would be considered depriving a local citizen of an opportunity for a good job. American families are diligent about ensuring their helpers are hired by another family when they depart the country and are known for treating their helpers well. Through the grapevine, we were connected with Khun Tan, a married mom of two daughters, originally from Isaan province in the northeast of Thailand. We arranged for her to work during the days, but not to live in the maid quarters, a very tiny space, as she lived nearby with her family. Khun Tan rode her bike to our house daily, using an umbrella or adjusting her travel time when needed to account for the weather. She was a jovial and kind woman who enjoyed making meals so spicy Vince's nose would run, and she found the boys entertaining. My long hours, much of which were spent commuting, kept me out of the house a lot and Khun Tan provided a great comfort to me in knowing the family would be fed on time and, let's be honest, that the toilets would be clean. The only thing ever noticeable in a toilet was the periodic appearance of a tiny gecko, which could be anywhere. Again, you get used to it and they help keep bugs away.

Initially, I struggled with the idea of being 'worthy' of such a luxury. I had been born into different life circumstances than Khun Tan, i.e., in America, but I did not view myself as above

her, or anyone else for that matter. My childhood, while humble
to some in America, still provided opportunity not available to
a woman born in a poor province in a developing country. Khun
Tan would sometimes outdo herself, going so far as to neatly fold
and arrange our socks and underwear drawers. I think I was also
a bit uncomfortable with such clear evidence of someone in the
private areas of our home, beyond basic cleaning.

Gradually, as I got to know Khun Tan, it became clear she
took great pride in her work and was committed doing a good job.
I was grateful to have her with us, caring for my family when I
worked late and making sure dinner was ready for Vince and the
kids. She saved us money on groceries, shopping locally rather
than at the neighborhood expat grocery store and introduced
everyone to new foods. Khun Tan periodically made fresh spring
rolls because she knew I liked to take them to work for my lunch.
She liked to test Vince's increasing spice tolerance, amping it
up and watching him sniffle through dinner. It was customary
to give bonuses on holidays, same as in the U.S., which we did.
When Khun Tan traveled home to Isaan, we always sent gifts of
outgrown family clothing and toys for the village. The head of
the village, like a mayor, would ensure we were treated to fresh
fruit each time Khun Tan returned.

Khun Tan was aware that we were trying to adopt a Thai
child. Like many Thai people, who struggled to support their
natural born families, it was a bit of a perplexing idea for her. She
used the word "lucky" whenever the topic came up. Khun Tan was
married, although we never met her husband. Her two daughters
periodically came to see her, and she would, initially, try to make
them invisible to us. Always one to ensure people feel seen, I made

sure she understood they were welcome any time. They joined in the neighborhood fun on Halloween, which was huge in the city. Imagine the perceived luxury of people just opening their doors to friends and complete strangers, giving away American and European candies and chocolates, which were expensive imports in Southeast Asia.

Prior to leaving the United States, we had celebrated Quinn's birthday early, so that he could be with his American friends. One month after moving abroad, we celebrated on his actual birthday. I was excited to show Quinn photos of his prior celebration with his friends in the U.S. He burst into tears upon seeing them and I was reminded of the internal stress on the kids despite the smiles on the outside. Vince and I were each settling into our new roles. I was up early each morning to commute to the Station while he adjusted to domestic life in a foreign country. Less than one month earlier, he had turned in his badge and gun and sold his diesel pickup truck, all within a single week. I was amazed and proud of his outward resilience and the support he provided us all.

Approximately two months after arrival in Southeast Asia, tragedy struck our family, but spared our lives. We returned home in our golf cart from a baseball game at the International School, as had quickly become the routine. Almost immediately, Vince realized something wasn't right. Our smoke alarms were going off and, when he opened the back door to the kitchen, he was met with a wall of black smoke. The gap between that discovery and the appearance of others coming to assist is a bit of a blur. A single police officer and one neighborhood employee arrived on scooters. The residential staffer, without shoes or any protective gear, determined from which window the bulk of the smoke was coming, climbed up a ladder armed only with a fire extinguisher, entered our sons' bedroom, and put out the fire.

Our boys lost almost every physical possession they brought with them to the other side of the world. The pile of stuffed animals that provided security and normalcy was completely gone. A dehumidifier had malfunctioned and combusted in their room, burned everything within a few feet, and ruined virtually everything in the house with smoke and soot. We had no idea how to begin to recover from this, but our faith was strong, and we knew that we would. Within a couple of hours, neighbors we barely knew, if at all, began appearing at our house, offering every kind of assistance you can imagine. The first couple to arrive, fellow Americans assigned to the embassy who had kids of their own, asked "Do your kids have pajamas and underwear to wear tonight?" I thought for a second and said, "They have nothing," still in a state of shock and not fully processing what I was saying. Next came a U.S. military officer, asking us to give him some of our clothing to begin trying to salvage what we could. Our neighbors across the street, a generous and kind family of five, took us in for the evening as the complex identified an alternative residence for us. Over the next several weeks, they also helped us in the aftermath. They hosted us for Thanksgiving and really contributed to the feeling of community and support. We are forever indebted for their kindness and empathy.

The next day, we were informed of where we would be staying while it was determined how to proceed with the house. We took the few usable things we had left and 'moved' to an apartment complex within the compound. We had not yet purchased a vehicle and the four of us drove to the apartment in our golf cart. As we pulled up in front of the building, Quinn said, holding back tears, "I feel sad." When we entered the apartment, we found others had been there before us to make it feel like home. They had placed stuffed animals throughout the apartment and filled the shelves with book and toys. A meal train was formed and, every day for two months, a different family arrived at the apartment at dinner time with a full meal for our entire family. The community and consistency of support we felt from former strangers provided comfort that is difficult to articulate. Buying groceries in a foreign country is different than at home and many familiar items are either expensive or hard to come by since they must be imported. The local Girl Scout troop collected donations for our family and packages of replacement items poured in from both family and friends in the U.S. and local colleagues who had only recently met us. My office was more than understanding and extended grace as our family pushed through this unexpected challenge. It's a strange and uncomfortable feeling when the helpers need help.

When Vince and I finally decided to go see the room where the fire had occurred, the boys' bedroom, it took my breath away. The same space they had chosen to share together as a place of safety and security in a foreign country, where they had put all their favorite things that provided them comfort, was now a charred, black mess. The white tiled bathroom was completely black, as was anything that had not burned. If you've never touched anything covered in soot, the particles are so small that they permeate every item with which they come into contact. Even washing things does not fully remove the forever changed feeling of the object. In this moment, I first felt horror, and then gratitude. I gave thanks to God that this tragedy had not occurred when we were sleeping and that all that was lost were material possessions.

For some time after the fire, the boys were understandably concerned it would happen again. Any beeping sound, such as the coffee maker, prompted anxiety. Even at six and seven years old, they were self-conscious about wearing donated uniforms and wearing backpacks that were not their own. We validated their feelings of loss and, concurrently, highlighted our blessings. We explained that, while this was a tragic experience for our family, we would be able to recover and to replace material things. We reminded them of the poverty just outside the gates of our neighborhood and how such an event would be catastrophic for some. On the other hand, we needed to help them get through this. We showed the boys it is okay to ask for and to accept help when you need it. Then, whenever you can be the helper, you do that. You do *what* you can *when* you can.

Taking this to heart, I modeled strength and grace for the kids during the day. I cried at night after they went to bed. I needed to give myself space to grieve and to release my own emotions from watching my kids go through this and having realized what could have happened. While the sight of the room had taken my breath away, I got it back. We were all still breathing. Each night, I soaked item after item in large bins of detergent and water to see what could be saved. Even items that said 'dry clean only' were immersed in the bins of soapy water to see if they would hold up. Survival of the fittest, so to speak. As I doused the clothes in and out of the water, tears of grief and gratitude flowed with each stroke. Ultimately, what mattered was that *we* had been saved.

Having moved into the apartment, it was unclear where we would next move for permanent housing. The compound had no available houses. We were offered the option to move back into our prior house once it was remediated from fire and smoke damage. Having seen the level to which soot seeps into everything, we didn't feel comfortable with that idea, as we pictured the air ducts and vents. Two colleagues, who had been serving in Southeast Asia for more than a couple of years, stepped up to help us. Since their kids had grown up and moved back to the U.S., they offered to move into a condominium downtown, an idea which had interested them for some time given their new lifestyle as empty nesters. As parents, they understood the value of security for their kids and had appreciated living in the neighborhood themselves. They moved into the city and freed up what had been their home to allow us to serve out our two years in a house as a family. It was a gracious act that was impactful in helping us move forward and we will always be deeply appreciative for their compassion and generosity.

Once we moved back into a house, the boys again shared a room, situated in the same place in the house as the last one. We decorated one bedroom to be a guest room, in hopes we would have guests and, later, another bedroom to be ready for a potential daughter and sister, or two. Over the course of the two years in Southeast Asia, we were visited by my longtime friend and former field hockey teammate, and her mother, and another time by my father. Southeast Asia is far and expensive and foreign, and not many people have the desire, resources, and internal fortitude to make such a trip. We were grateful for those who did visit, and to share this life-changing experience with loved ones.

We had several opportunities to get out of the city to visit neighboring towns that were significantly different from the hustle and bustle of downtown. There were multiple beaches within two to three hours' drive that many expatriates and locals alike would visit. Other popular beaches in Southeast Asia such as Phuket and Krabi required a flight, one of which we visited while my friend and her mom were traveling in the region. The views are famous for their splendor, and we saw live versions of beautiful postcards. We took elephant rides, drank from coconuts, and ate the most delicious foods. With Southeast Asian heritage in my friend's family, we all enjoyed sharing a portion of their journey.

During our vacation travels, we learned other elements of Thai culture. Thai people greet others with a gesture called a wai (pronounced 'why'). A proper Thai wai involves putting the hands together, fingers pointing straight up, much like prayer hands and leaning forward in a slight bow to show respect. The placement of the top of the fingers is relative to the appropriate level of respect. The higher on the body the fingertips are placed, the more respect displayed. For example, greeting a senior Thai official would prompt one to place the fingertips closer to the forehead whereas greeting a peer would have the hands down around the chest. If you ever met a member of the Royal Thai Family, the bow would also become deeper. Once Americans get the hang of the wai, we tend to almost overdo it, including with servers in restaurants, until Thai friends clarify what is appropriate.

Another Thai custom is the use of a preceding particle in addressing others. The word 'Khun', pronounced 'koon', as used earlier in describing Khun Tan, is used in front of someone's first name, even for senior officials and those with some rank. It is a custom to show respect and is extended to everyone. We were referred to by Thai acquaintances as 'Khun Holly', 'Khun Vince', 'Khun Boston', and 'Khun Quinn'. The word is used in greeting people both in person and in writing, such as emails, and regardless of gender. All Thai people are also given a nickname when they are babies. They tend to be one or two syllables, almost always simpler to spell and pronounce than the given Thai name, which tends to be multiple syllables. Nicknames sometimes have special meaning, and other times are more fun and lighthearted. Even in using nicknames, Thai people include the preceding 'Khun', for example, 'Khun Kwan'.

In researching Thai adoption, I discovered that in Thailand there is no financial subsidy provided for food, such as food stamps in the U.S. So, if a person or couple are unable to provide or appropriately care for their child, their option is to take them to a publicly funded orphanage. It is generally considered temporary care, and sometimes it is. Often, however, children remain in these residential facilities for years. Our understanding was that, if a birth parent or relative returned to the orphanage once per year to sign a paper saying they still wished to have their child stay in temporary care, the child was not eligible for adoption. I did not hear of any time limit on this arrangement. While heartbreaking to consider giving up one's child, it might be logical after some years, if a person realized they would not be able to or did not want to bring the child back home, to ultimately sign away their parental rights. I learned from my research that, in Thai culture, doing so causes the parent or relative to feel a 'loss of face' which is a loss of respect or feeling of humiliation.

I had heard it was frowned upon by the Thai government to volunteer at orphanages and potentially try to 'choose' your child. As a result, I had intentionally avoided visiting any of the government-run orphanages in and around Bangkok. There were more than 20 such orphanages throughout the country. On a beach vacation to Pattaya in Thailand, we prearranged a visit to a private orphanage to spend some time with the children and offer some donations. It was spacious and well-kept. They were accustomed to receiving visitors as they relied on donations and funding from non-government sources. We entered a large room full of older infants and toddlers, all spread out in metal cribs. There were so many beautiful children, and our hearts were immediately touched. The Thai kids all clamored for our attention as we spread throughout the room to greet them. Thailand has a very loving culture and it's simply a numbers game of way more children than caregivers, leaving the kids always wanting more.

Because most of the caregivers in orphanages are female, the children see a fewer number of men in their young lives. As Vince moved through the room, the little boys reached out for him. I remember him holding one little boy who simply did not want to let go. This room was full of children we had never met, and I loved every one of them. There were triplets with an older sister and my heart longed to bring them home. I knew it was not logistically feasible, both according to process and because we already had two children. We felt it was more than we could take on to even pursue it. But what I knew after that visit was that we had the capacity to love whatever child was meant for our family.

Another trip took us northwest of Bangkok to a rural area called Kanchanaburi where we visited the 'bridge over the River Kwai' (of the famed movie by the same name) and an elephant rescue sanctuary. We were picked up at our hotel by a Thai man in an old pickup truck, hopped in the back, and rode many miles into the country. For me, it was reminiscent of a 1970s childhood adventure, not uncommon on the Eastern Shore of Maryland when I was a kid. It was initially a little scary with our two little boys along for the ride, but as we breathed in the unpolluted, country air and saw the miles and miles of nature around us, it was exhilarating. We were grateful for the boys to have this experience, which would never happen in 21st century America, at least in and around Washington, D.C.

On this trip, we had the opportunity to learn about and care for elephants, riding bare back into the river, along with their caretakers ('mahouts'), washing the elephants, cooking rice and mango in giant vats, shaping the mixture into softball-sized snacks, and hand-feeding the elephants. Most of the elephants took the rice ball with their trunks and put it into their mouths themselves. However, one elderly elephant was unable to do so, and I was able to put the ball directly into her mouth. We learned that elephants are one of the animal species who will adopt other elephants outside their family who need care and there was one such 'family' at the rescue. This was especially touching and meaningful given our quest to adopt.

With our church, and while my father was visiting, we traveled to a Burmese refugee village within Thailand to help install flooring in their rustic school structures. We traveled in the used Honda CR-V we had purchased from Japan, a common practice for expatriates seeking a good deal on a well-maintained car while serving in Southeast Asia. There was something about the smell of the car that repulsed Vince and the boys. There wasn't a specific foul smell, just an unpleasant odor of some sort that often gave them headaches, and exacerbated Quinn's periodic car sickness. Fortunately, I drove the car most often and was less affected by it. On this trip, we stopped to get gas and barely got Quinn out of the car fast enough for him to vomit all over the concrete in front of the gas pump. We looked up to see every Thai person within view staring as he finished. I shrugged, cleaned him up while Vince pumped the gas, and on we continued.

At the camp, it was intended for the refugees to be in Thailand temporarily, until they were safely able to return to Burma (referred to internally as Myanmar). However, the refugees had already been in Thailand for multiple years and were restricted to a defined area. They had been displaced due to their Christian faith. Burma is predominantly Buddhist, with Buddhism being generally a peaceful religion. However, in Burma, the Christian population is heavily persecuted.

It was a special day that again showed the power of a smile, food, and hard work in bringing people together. The boys played with the Burmese children and helped the other boys and adults work. I did a craft project with some of the girls, and we were all treated to the finest feast the village could provide, simple, but one of the most meaningful meals in my lifetime. It was incredibly powerful to be in this humble space with the refuge residents, giving of our time, receiving their amazing hospitality and gratitude, and praying for positive developments. As we departed, it was pouring rain. In the distance, I heard the distinct sound of a newborn cry. I was overcome by the difficulty these mothers faced, giving birth in the forest, in a foreign land, unsure what the future held. My tears were washed away as the rained pounded, but the memory is seared in my mind and on my heart forever.

A family trip took us to a place called Safari World. It was an exotic wildlife park that visitors drove through. As we entered the gates, in our car, the first gate closed behind us before the second gate opened. After passing through the second gate, we were within the confines of the habitat of lions, zebras, tigers, and other animals. Throughout the park, staff members patrolled in small vehicles that looked like the old Suzuki Samurai, painted to look like zebras, and periodically revved their engines to coax the animals to back away from the road as patrons drove through. I laugh as I remember this, because some of the best experiences in Thailand were things that would never be allowed in the U.S. for legal and liability reasons. They were so exciting and freeing; ironic, coming from the Land of Freedom to the Land of Smiles, as Thailand is known.

In addition to our travels to Thailand, we had the opportunity to travel to Australia. Quinn's favorite animal had always been the koala and we knew this was potentially our once in a lifetime opportunity to visit their home. We split our travel between the metropolitan area of Sydney, a small town that housed a koala hospital, and a rural area ('the bush') that was home to Aboriginal people. It was important to me that we be exposed to and honor the culture of the Aborigines, as Australia continued to grapple with racial tensions and discrimination, like the U.S. We attended a cultural presentation and visited national landmarks. We bounced from an Airbnb in a cottage behind a kind woman's house, to a motel whose website pictures were apparently outdated, to the tiniest two hotel rooms I have ever seen. Getting in and out of the restrooms in our closet rooms was a challenge, but all worth it to see the New Year's Eve fireworks over the Sydney Opera House. On top of that, one of my old friends, and former roommate, was living in Australia with her family. We had not seen each other in years, and we met up to ring in the new year.

Whenever we visited new places, including Australia, we would always buy a small gift for our future daughter. These material things, such as a canvas rendering of an Aboriginal piece of artwork, are still in her room now; reminders that, even when she was not physically with us, she was in our hearts and on our minds. It is a strange realization, guilt-provoking, that we saw more of Thailand in two years in Southeast Asia than she did in her five years there, even though she was young and would not have remembered much of it. Nonetheless, she has more Thailand *in* her than we could ever see or visit. Geography and culture are not the same thing.

As much as I love Thailand and adore Thai people, I would not be true to myself or this story if I didn't acknowledge that Bangkok has a dark side, which added to my motivation to stay the course on the adoption process. I presume the shady side also exists in other parts of Thailand, and Southeast Asia, but I can only speak from the perspective of what I personally witnessed or heard about from others. There is an underworld of sex, drugs, and human trafficking that is not so hidden if you are out at certain times or in certain areas. Sadly, much of this dark side is fueled by a steady stream of non-Thai tourists who come from all over the world to experience it. While many of these things occur in many major cities throughout the world, including the U.S., this city mattered more to me. Bangkok, Thailand was not just another city in some country. It was the city and country from which my daughter would originate and presumably already had.

Seeing the dark side prompted deep reflection about beliefs and opportunities. I remember once walking through the city while on vacation and thinking I felt the absence of God. My faith quickly took over and my next thought was, "No. God is here. They just don't know Him." Thailand's population is over 90% Buddhist with a small percentage of other religions including Christianity and Islam. Buddhism is a peaceful religion with positive messages. Its nonconfrontational principles, however, overlaid by Thai culture on a broader scale, allow certain things to continue that could potentially be addressed more directly than they are. As for other religions, I was caught by surprise the first time I heard the Muslim call to prayer while relaxing at the neighborhood pool back home, from which I could also view the Christian church we attended. It was in that church that we discovered the true beauty of faith. We worshipped with people from all over the world, literally, and it was they who took up the sword to feed our family and help us salvage what we could after the fire.

Some of the sights in downtown Bangkok physically felt like a kick in the gut. Children were often sighted in various scenarios that required steeling of my emotions to stomach. The most common example was the routine sight of a woman holding a 'sleeping' child while begging for money. Unsuspecting tourists regularly fill their cups while expatriates who live in Thailand are advised not to do so as it was almost always part of a money-making ruse to pull on one's heart strings. The children were said to be drugged, presumably with something mild such as cough medicine, and were not necessarily the child of the present adult. Another common sight was an amputee, sliding along the concrete in the center of the city, pushing a tin cup with his face. Heartbreaking. Rumor had it that the ringleaders would drop off these people around town and then later pick them up, along with whatever money had been collected.

I once turned a street corner to see an older sibling tending to a younger sibling who was laying on a makeshift bed on the sidewalk. More than once, I choked back tears and kept walking. In Bangkok, people mind their own business. Thai people have a unique and well-developed ability to maintain a sense of harmony in keeping with Buddhist tradition. There is both acceptance of some things as 'normal' and a refusal to outwardly react to sometimes disturbing situations. It is easy for tourists to judge and question Thai culture. However, people the world over, including in the U.S., also turn a blind eye to injustices right in front of them and do not always act when they could. Before casting judgment, look in the mirror. Look around. Lead from where you are.

It sounds crazy now, but I couldn't help but imagine if I could scoop up one or more of these children and give them a different life. I quickly answered myself with reality and logic. This was home for each of these kids and, even if it was possible to pay someone for a child, I could not legally bring them home, and they probably would not want to leave their home anyway. Home is home, no matter where it is. I had learned that in our first foster/adoption training.

Each time I saw such a scenario, it fueled my fire to bring home our daughter, who would otherwise have limited opportunities coming out of an orphanage. No one can do everything, but everyone can do something. We were doing something. Our daughter had been born worthy of love, belonging, and the opportunity to become all that she is meant to. We were committed to providing that opportunity. God was always there, and still is, sustaining the children who wait and filling the hearts of those who seek Him.

CHAPTER 6

Thailand's Adoption Process

With big goals, and sometimes even smaller ones, it's the start that stops most people. Despite all the challenges faced up to this point in our efforts to adopt, I remained committed to it and resolute in pressing on. Now, living in Southeast Asia, I had the benefit of Thai colleagues and partners who could assist me in understanding and communicating with Thai adoption authorities. Additionally, there was another American Embassy family who had been involved in the adoption process for some time. Following guidance and my heart, I began the paperwork to adopt a Thai child. I still did not understand that we were initially beginning a Thai adoption process which, if our daughter had been placed with us before departing Southeast Asia, would have required us to either relocate to Thailand for three years (which was not an option) or to leave her behind and return later to Thailand to bring her home (an unappealing option).

Not long after submitting initial paperwork, our Thai social worker, Khun Achara, contacted us to conduct a home study. During the interview, she asked us what age was preferred. Sticking with our prior agreement not to seek an infant or toddler and wanting to increase our chances of receiving a placement, we said two to six years old. We also agreed to the possibility of sibling sisters. Khun Achara asked us if we would consider a child older than six to which we responded affirmatively but noted our preference to maintain birth order. She then asked if we would consider a child under two years old. Vince and I looked at each other, silently communicating years of discussions in a single moment. Our knowing gaze affirmed our agreement that we would rather not revisit the infant or toddler stage, but that what we really wanted was to adopt a child and did not want to do anything to decrease our chances of a match. I looked back at Khun Achara and answered that we would be open to a child under two. We wanted to keep the door open to whatever child was meant for our family.

Ultimately, in true Thai fashion of honoring specific criteria, we would be matched with an almost four-year-old girl, smack dab in the middle of our stated range. At the time of our required Thai adoption home study, unbeknownst to us or to Khun Achara, our future daughter was about two and a half years old, living a short flight from our Southeast Asian residence. We would not meet her for another three years.

It was exciting to start the adoption process from within Southeast Asia. We were hopeful that it would move along faster because we were in the region, which proved false. There were months between each step. Even with the help of Thai colleagues and partners assisting with the personal delivery of documents and asking follow-up questions to ensure no miscommunications, we felt uncertain about whether it was going to happen. As an official family living abroad, you rely almost exclusively on the embassy mail pouch system for letters and packages to and from the U.S. and even locally. In the case of our Thai adoption process, we preferred to hand carry all documents to ensure delivery confirmation that we would otherwise not receive. It meant too much to us to take any risk regarding the paperwork, even though the adoption itself could be considered one big risk. It was during this time that my commitment to the process solidified. I had mantras that kept me going. "Just keep putting the ball back in their court." "Don't let you be what's holding you back." "If not us, then whom?"

The process of gathering so many documents is daunting, and necessary. The Thai dossier package required for international adoptions mirrors that of many other countries that are part of the Hague Adoption Convention. We were required to submit the following things.

- Application of Child Adoption
- Letter of Intent
- Home Study Report by licensed agency (in this case Thai authorities)
- Birth Certificate of both parents (certified original documents)
- Marriage Certificate (certified original document)
- Divorce or Death Decrees (*if applicable*)
- Alien Resident "Green Card" (*if applicable*)
- Medical Letter for each parent
- Letter from a medical professional, if on any prescribed medication, chronic medical condition, etc.

- Letter documenting infertility or other reason pregnancy is not advisable (*if applicable*)
- Psychological Evaluation Report for each parent
- Certificate of Net Worth
- Front page of the last two 1040 income tax returns
- Two letters from a bank, credit union, or other financial institution
- Employment, Self-Employment, and/or Homemaker Letters for each parent
- Police clearance statement for each parent (in our case, the Royal Thai Police)
- USCIS I800A Approval
- Two letters of recommendation
- Copy of passport for each parent
- Agreement to register your child with the Thai Consulate in the U.S.
- Promise to finalize the adoption in the US
- Verification of adoption education

All the documents above were required to be notarized or, in the case of vital records, certified copies.

The dossier also included the following items which did not need to be notarized.

- Five identical passport photos of each parent
- Nine recent pictures – three of our immediate family, three of the outside of the home, and three of the inside of the home
- Post-Adoption Agreement (three home-study visits in the new country over at least six months and results forwarded to the Thai authorities)
- Inter-agency agreement (provide annual updates via the home country adoption agency to the Thai adoption

agency to maintain a positive intercountry adoption partnership)

As we moved through the processing, including a visit to the
Royal Thai Police Headquarters for fingerprinting, rudimentary
Thai language allowed me to ingratiate myself. However, a smile
is key to connecting within the Land of Smiles. There were multiple times that I visited Thai government entities with complete
dependence on the documents in my hand to explain why I was
there, and trust in fellow human beings to help me through a
process that I was not sure they supported. They always came
through. Being the antsy American, I would periodically ask my
Thai friends to check in for us on the process. We were neither
asking for favoritism nor trying to get around any requirements,
but rather to ensure we understood the state of the process and
that it was, in fact, continuing. It was a constant internal battle
to trust the process and required a continued focus on faith.

At times, Vince or I would grow weary, unsure if we were
doing the right thing for our family, or if it would ever really
work out. Vince struggled to commit emotionally, afraid of potential heartbreak and disappointment. Late one evening, standing
in our kitchen, having yet another discussion about adoption,
Vince expressed his concerns – about the process taking so long,
whether we should continue, and whether we would know if the
time came to abandon the quest. My strong feeling was that, if we
were meant to stop trying to adopt, it would somehow be made
very clear to us. I implored Vince to think beyond the process,
the paperwork, and the appointments, and focus instead on the
human being on the other side of all of that, probably just a short
flight away; to consider the outcome, if we stayed the course. I

repeated that she was likely not all that far away. Given we were adopting an 'older' child, I found it helpful to remember she was already out there, and I wondered what she looked like. It kept me going. Vince cried as he allowed his heart to feel. The thought of her together with our family kept us both going and allowed us to remain committed to the process, taking each step as we could, rather than fixating on the outcome seeming so far away.

As part of our adoption processing, we were required to attend adoption training in Thailand. There was one session for Thai adoptive parents, which often consisted of other Thai family members, and one session for non-Thai adoptive parents. Our classmates included people from Europe, Australia, South Africa, and fellow Americans. Some families already had a child placed with them while others, like us, were waiting anxiously to get to that point. One of the speakers was introduced as the perfect spokesperson for the process of which we were all a part. As he walked into the room, his physical stature was marked in its difference from the standard Thai male. He was taller and more muscular than most, although there are plenty of physically fit Thai men, and he exuded confidence that belied his American identity. As he spoke, I felt immense pride at what an American family had done for this impressive young man. He, too, expressed complete adoration for his parents – all his parents, including biological, foster, and adoptive.

This young man had recently returned to Thailand to teach English and get in touch with his birth culture. He had met with his foster parents, and he also planned to meet his birth mother, but was not yet ready. He spoke about having been adopted into the primarily white U.S. Midwest and the challenges he had faced. Still, his clear and heartfelt message to all of us was "Keep going. You're doing a great thing." Knowing every adoption story is unique, I was nonetheless even more firmly resolute about our efforts after hearing from this young man, whom the Thai social worker described as having "Thai hardware with American software".

After leaving the training session, I reflected on what it must have been like to be adopted into a family who was likely unfamiliar with one's birth culture and probably had little to no access to Thai cultural exposure. Having visited the Thai Embassy in Washington, D.C., and Wat Thai DC, I felt grateful that we would have opportunities to support our daughter's connection to her Thai cultural heritage. Frequent visits to and vacations in Thailand, too, provided our entire family an education and insight into Thai culture. We all spoke some basic Thai. The boys were studying Thai language at the International School, and Vince had taken it upon himself to take some lessons.

Thai people are generally polite and calm. They love children and are often non-confrontational. Knowing how they adore children was comforting when considering that our daughter was somewhere in an orphanage. In Thailand, that was a significantly less dire situation than in many other countries. We knew that, wherever our future daughter was, she was loved. It was not in the same way as a traditional family, but it was family, nonetheless.

Thai culture is deeply rooted in a long history, dating back almost 800 years since its founding. Thai people are proud to say their country was never colonized. Thai culture draws on influences from neighboring countries such as India and China whose impact is seen in food and clothing. Thai temples are ornate in design, and it is a high crime to speak ill of the Thai monarchy. Many Thai products have a youthful graphic depiction in their presentation and advertising. However, formal presentations are more traditionally regal. And no one does pomp and circumstance better than the Thai people. Ribbons, bows, and lots of gold. I smile when I think of celebrations in Thailand. My daughter's spirit was formed in this setting.

Before we knew it, our two years in Southeast Asia was nearing its end, amid ongoing political crisis. Two months prior to our scheduled departure, the Royal Thai Armed Forces launched a coup d'état, at least the 10th such event in Thailand's history, depending upon documentation perspective. It was wild to experience this from nearby and see it play out in many ways including a Thai government takeover of news channels with nationwide addresses to announce that a military junta had been formed to rule as an interim government. Once again, the more peaceful nature of the Thai culture kept this upheaval at a level somewhat less dramatic than many other countries. In some protest areas, music blared, and fresh fruit and t-shirts were sold to passersby. The U.S. government had supported the recently overthrown democratic government. Consequently, there were protests outside U.S. Embassy Bangkok, but people were generally kept away from the main gates by security. We were never quite sure if the local security forces would've stood tall in the face of a true embassy attack, but, we generally felt safe when visiting Thailand post-coup. I did, however, wear an 'Australia' t-shirt out in public, when not traveling to the embassy, to deflect any potential negative attention. Sometimes it's better to move in silence.

Meanwhile, we continued preparations to return home to the U.S. We had not yet been matched with our daughter and we felt an ache at the prospect of leaving Southeast Asia without her. We feared being so far away and possibly forgotten in the process. I made one last visit to speak with our Thai social worker, Khun Achara, before departing for the other side of the world. It was unannounced, which was a slightly rude choice, but I knew it was the only way I'd likely get to speak with her. The Thai social workers have a heavy case load and generally only contact you if there is something new to share or something needed in your file. Khun Achara was gracious although likely annoyed. I reiterated our commitment to adopt a Thai daughter and ensured that we each had accurate contact information for the other.

A British friend from church accompanied me and provided much needed moral support. She was a tangible reminder of our faith in God and His ability to bring us together with the child meant for our family and us for the child. She was one of many Christians we met at the local community Christian church. Worshipping with a global congregation was one of the most humbling and joy-filled experiences of my time in Southeast Asia. Having a church-mate make this final stop with me, out of the sheer goodness of her heart and her commitment to Thai orphans, which was her daily endeavor while living in Thailand, felt symbolic of the global connection of Christians, since it was church that had brought us together. I'm so grateful to have experienced it firsthand and will forever appreciate her quiet support and encouragement to keep the faith.

It was hard to believe the time had seemingly come and gone so quickly. While Vince and I had hoped for both of us to be working and to reap some of the financial benefits of living abroad, things hadn't worked out that way. Vince had not worked while in Southeast Asia but gained so much more than money during our time there. Having been on multiple Presidential detail assignments before we moved overseas, and missed so many events with the kids, this tour had given him back that time. He had been the boys' coach, swimming instructor, and primary support while I worked. He had made a forever friend in a Dutch physical therapist and personal trainer, for and with whom Vince worked. In their down time, they went fishing for 'river monsters' multiple times.

As we prepared to return home to the U.S., we made last minute purchases of Southeast Asian souvenirs including a 'Sawatdi kha lady'. In Thailand, you see her outside of many restaurants and businesses. At our home in the U.S., she greets you as you enter and depart, with a proper Thai wai. I think most Thai people would find it curious, maybe funny, but then quickly chalk it up to farangs being farangs.

CHAPTER 7

Coming Home Without Her

In almost every way, we resumed life back in the U.S. as it was before our time abroad. We moved back into the same house, which we had rented out while abroad, and the boys returned to the same school. They were thrilled to see familiar faces and teachers. The house was still home. Meanwhile, we waited. Although still not matched, every decision included consideration of our daughter. The boys shared the larger bedroom again, so that we could prepare the smaller room for their future sister. It was a natural follow on to having previously shared the room and to having shared a bedroom while overseas. They were now two years older, and we still wanted to ensure they did not associate sharing a bedroom with gaining a sister.

The time between deciding to adopt and having a new child enter one's home is long. It is much longer than pregnancy and is sometimes called a 'paper pregnancy'. Despite the biological difference, the space allows time for preparing one's heart and mind for the significant change and transition that will occur. Like delivering a child, though, no amount of mental and emotional preparation is quite the same as the real thing. You cannot predict how the child will react. Imagining scenarios, however, can be helpful, as with visualizing for sports or other performance-based activity. Your brain doesn't know the difference between real and imagined, so when the time comes, it's as though you've been there before. When I was pregnant with Quinn, I would imagine putting two kids into the car seats as I strapped in Boston. Or, as I was carrying baby gear, I would consider how I would manage two kids and the gear at the same time. When it came to imagining life with a third child, who was not a baby, but was significantly younger than we had experienced in several years, I didn't realize just how much attention it would take. It was difficult to visualize the scenarios and I imagined our daughter needing less help than she did. Despite all the adoption training, in the U.S. and the Thai processes, the developmental gaps and delays would ultimately be new to me and all of us.

We needed two vehicles since we did not have any when we returned from abroad. Retrofitting our Japanese purchased Honda to have a left side steering wheel would have been too costly to undertake…and that smell. We were sure to get at least one vehicle that was large enough to transport three to four kids. I researched our childcare options and tried to calculate (guess) at what point to put ourselves on a waiting list, if the facility would allow it, for a child not having been identified yet and without a name for enrollment. As difficult as it was to stay focused on the end goal while remaining committed to the process, it was even more challenging to keep others informed and have them truly believe with you. We were met with a mix of empathetic comments about the length of the process and sometimes silent, sometimes not, judgment about the decision to adopt. I found it helpful to post updates on social media to spread the word while shielding me from potentially negative feedback from in-person conversations or potentially having to repeat myself over and over.

Having returned to the U.S., I learned we were now required to insert an American adoption agency to help manage the process. This also meant significantly higher costs and giving up direct communication with the Thai government. The fees related to adoption of a Thai child were less than those for several other countries, but several thousand dollars, nonetheless. Prospective adoptive parents often have fundraisers of all sorts to help finance the administrative costs associated with adoption of a child. I began by examining the costs.

There were only a handful of American adoption agencies that helped American families adopt Thai children. The process was less straightforward than some other countries, so I chose the one that seemed the most experienced in adoptions, writ large, both domestic and from various countries internationally. The choice was based solely on my belief that experience matters. Although, another agency might argue that specialized experience matters more. I have no doubt the other agencies are competent, too, but I went with what felt right to me.

I inquired with the agency about the cost breakdown. I requested an itemized list of the fees, given I had already done a significant amount of work and processing on my own while living in Southeast Asia. I was confident that some of the costs would be for things I had already done directly with the Thai government. Once I received the list, I negotiated together with the agency to get the fees down to what we all felt was fair after crossing off steps I had already completed. Part of signing on with the American adoption agency was an agreement to cease direct contact with the Thai government. We had not yet signed that agreement as we were still negotiating terms.

Vince and I had another heart-to-heart about the continued pursuit of adoption. He expressed concern that perhaps it was no longer the right path for us. The frustrations of repeated home studies, including interviews, doctor visits, and more paperwork, take a toll and allow time for doubt to slip in. Vince wondered if the money spent on yet another home study update would be more appropriately directed toward the boys, the very real children we already had. For so long, the process is very much a one-way street. You give time and money with little to no encouragement along the way, not unlike those grueling early days of having a newborn, particularly for dads who often anxiously await the opportunity to play with the kid. It is an exercise in faith and determination. As a fiercely determined person who has great vision for the possible, I continued to believe our daughter was out there already. I was not ready to give up.

Same as always, I expressed my belief that, if we were meant to change course, it would be made very clear to us. It would not be ambiguous. It was too important of a life choice. Truly a 'life' choice, for several people. I believed that something of the magnitude of the expiration of our D.C. adoption certification would occur if we were not meant to adopt. The conversation prompted me to send an email to Khun Achara, while I still could, having not yet signed the agreement to cease communication.

Vince and I visited multiple local churches of various denominations looking for one that provided the same warmth and feel of our neighborhood church overseas. We settled on one based on the pastor, Reverend Rachel, and the welcoming congregation. They offered an earlier, more casual service in a small chapel that suited having very young children and our preference for a 'come as you are' worship service. Periodically, we would attend the traditional services in the main sanctuary. This was the first time I had ever seen a pastor that 'looked like me'. Each week, the service felt like a friend sharing the Word. She often wore comfortable dresses with tights and boots, and cool earrings, as though we shared a closet. It showed me the power of being able to identify with a person in a position of respect and authority. The idea that, if you can see it, you can be it. While I wasn't pursuing a life of ministry, it felt like Rev. Rachel spoke directly to me and empowered me to keep shining my own light. She became a friend of the family and was supportive as we moved through the adoption process. Often when talking with people about adoption, you get a feeling they aren't sure it's ever really going to work out. With Rachel, I knew she believed, and it helped sustain me. There is so much power in kind words and being truly present for someone. Never underestimate your ability to positively impact the life of another.

CHAPTER 8

Match and Approval

About six months after returning to the U.S., I had sent that late night email to Khun Achara to touch base, following yet another heart-to-heart between Vince and I on the topic of adoption. As described, I had met face-to-face with Khun Achara in Thailand multiple times. I partly resented, but also understood the requirement to stop communications. I was sitting at the dining room table, which doubled as my work area, and I emailed Khun Achara to say hello and remind her we were still here, waiting and committed. I sent a photo of the boys playing in the snow. It doesn't snow in Thailand, although they do artificial snow well in Christmas displays. Because of the twelve-hour time difference, late night communications from the U.S. reach Thailand already in the morning hours of the following day; an afternoon email from Thailand arrives in the U.S. in the middle of the night. When I checked my email the following evening, there was a message in my inbox from Thailand. I opened the email with more anticipation than I had felt in quite some time related to the adoption. I skimmed the entire email as quickly as I could and had to calm myself to reread and process it.

"Dear Khun Vincent and Holly,

Thank you so much for your email and news. I'm also very glad to inform you that the Child Adoption Board has recently matched a girl aged about 3.10 years old from The Babies Home to your family. She was born on …"

Based on the date of birth and the mentioned age at the time of the match, the Board had matched us over two months prior. We had just not yet been notified, likely due to the standard heavy case load and holiday season. The mentioned orphanage was, in fact, less than 10 miles from one of our favorite family vacation spots in Thailand. She had been so close so often for the entire two years we were abroad. I read the email at least 10 times trying to take it in. I did some research on a mentioned medical condition and responded affirmatively to the social worker. I asked if they had a photo of the child. Vince and the boys were all in bed and I wanted desperately to wake up everyone and scream "We have a match!" But, without a picture, that would have been somewhat anticlimactic. The process really becomes the focus until such time that the outcome is within sight. It finally seemed it was.

Many details over the course of so many years of process are lost in our memories. Certain moments, though, are seared in my mind. That week, I was traveling for work. One evening in a hotel, I checked my email, hoping for a next response from Thailand. There it was. Khun Achara sent three photos of our matched child and my heart exploded at the sight of her sweet little face. She looked uncertain even in the photos including one in which she was displaying a halfhearted wai, fingers slightly bent. I wanted to jump through the screen to get to her and hold her. I forwarded the email to my husband and continued looking at the photos every chance I got. When I returned home from the trip, I saw that Vince had printed the photos of our future daughter and taped them on his bedside cabinet, near his Bible. This had been the very real and tangible sign he needed to stay the course. She was real.

After receiving word of being matched, it was ultimately another year and three months before we could get to her. We were allowed to send her small packages every two or three months. They had to fit within a gallon size Ziploc bag and were mailed to the adoption agency on the west coast of the U.S., who would then prepare them for onward shipment to Thailand. I presume the gallon bag was to make it easy to pack, as several were shipped together for various children, or it may have been to help parents control themselves from going overboard, or both. We usually sent one clothing item such as pajamas or a shirt, and a small toy or book. We still have the magnet version of 'paper doll' we sent, that later was a favorite toy of our daughter's while we were in Thailand to meet her and bring her home.

We were also able to send a family photo album to introduce our daughter to her new adoptive family. I was excited to work on it, thinking she would possibly feel comforted in seeing our smiles and happiness in the photos. I requested the assistance of a Thai-American colleague in writing the words 'father', 'mother', and 'brother' on paper signs that we each held in photos included in the books. We wanted to assist the caregivers in explaining who we were as they flipped through the book as we were unsure if they would be able to speak or read English. This album is still on a bookshelf in her room.

Yet another Christmas would go by without bringing her home. And before that, Mother's Day, Father's Day, July 4th (we celebrate it big!), Halloween, Thanksgiving, and her birthday. During that time, I stuck to my practice of always doing whatever was asked by the process, as quickly as possible, to put the ball back in the court of the process. I refused to ever be the cause of continued delays in bringing home our daughter. Always control what *you* can control.

As we waited, we began to consider names, including her given name and whether we would change it. What's in a name? This is an interesting question to consider for someone who has gone by many names throughout life based on personal and professional circumstances. By the time I married Vince, I was taking my third name, having had my birth father's last name, initially, followed by my stepfather's last name, so that I could 'match' the rest of the family, and finally, taking my husband's last name. As independent as I had always been, I had dreamed of marriage and proudly taking a last name that truly felt it was mine because it was that of a partner whom I'd chosen for myself.

My job, too, had required the use of different names for the protection of people and information. Even when I had chosen those, there had been meaning. Regardless of what name I'd used, I was still the same person. This was also true for many close colleagues whom I called friends. So, in a sense, a name may have little to do with identity but could also hold significant meaning. The important part is knowing who you are. For many of us, this stems from knowing our background, our origin, or so we think. All those things can also place external expectations on us of who we are supposed to be. Knowing your heritage cuts both ways. What is most critical in knowing who you are is knowing your values and what is most important to you, and why. You get to choose some of the most important parts of your identity.

For our daughter, we weren't sure what we would learn about her background or what was known. She had been given a beautiful Thai name meaning 'noble woman' by her caregivers at The Babies Home. Her last name had been chosen after a respected Thai Buddhist elder about whom I have been unable to find any English language history. Both names were compassionately selected to bestow upon her the dignity of which she is worthy. I knew that her Thai name would be mispronounced in English. While I like both the correctly pronounced and incorrectly pronounced versions, the inaccuracy of the American pronunciation had the potential to drive me crazy. We talked, as a family, about keeping her Thai name as a middle name, so that she could use it at any point she chose to and giving her a hybrid first name that also began with the letter 'J', which was the same as her Thai first name. As we discussed the topic at the dinner table, Boston thoughtfully offered a lovely name that has the 'J' sound but is usually spelled with a 'G' and has Italian versus Asian or American roots. We briefly pondered it because it was beautiful and then continued thinking.

As I did some research, I came upon the name 'Jessi', spelled without the traditional American 'e'. It is the Hindi version and means 'Gift from God'. Thailand has many cultural influences from both China and India and many differences from the U.S.

I found this name particularly meaningful as we believe she is a gift from God, a presence not always openly acknowledged in Thailand, but important in our family. In a way, the name blended two cultures and countries. It was not an uncommon name for a Thai woman as I found online, most of whom spelled it the Hindi way, not the commonly used American versions, male (Jesse) or female (Jessie). I suspected it might sometimes be misspelled in the U.S., but never mispronounced.

Our Jessi would already face a significant challenge in discovering who she is. However, her situation could also be looked at as having a blank canvas and no predetermined assumptions of her path. Alternatively, having a starting point without any parameters for proceeding might also be confusing and overwhelming. At a minimum, we would select for her a name which honored the value of her existence, our faith in God, and blended the two countries that would most heavily influence the shaping of her identity.

While we initially called Jessi by her Thai name in Thailand and for a period in the U.S., she is referred to herein by her American name for clarity and privacy.

One year later, I was working further into the evening than usual. There were few people in the office, and it was quiet. I had received a voicemail to call the adoption agency, located on the west coast. So, while it was after normal business hours on the east coast, it was late afternoon in Oregon. I made the call. The Board had approved our case and it was time to plan travel to bring home our daughter. I remember the layout of the office very clearly and where I was standing as I hung up the phone and let out a shriek of joy. The release I felt in that moment was akin to victory. Having worked hard for something that matters to you, putting in time, day after day, for a purpose bigger than oneself. Relying on faith and determination to keep you going even in the face of uncertainty. Relentless pursuit of that which you seek.

I was not completely alone in the office and a junior officer appeared at my doorway to make sure everything was okay. I didn't know him well and he was unfamiliar with the long journey on which my family and I had been up to this point. I shared with him the gist of what had just happened, knowing the gravity of the moment was lost on him, not by any fault of his own. While he and I have not kept up since each moving on to new assignments, that moment is seared in my mind forever and I would imagine in his too. A life lesson in persistence and faith.

It was almost unbelievable that, after all that time, it was finally time to book tickets to Thailand to meet and bring home our daughter – chosen for us, we believe, by divine purpose rather than by luck or by chance. All the emotions that had been held at bay for so long were finally appropriate to just feel without fear of disappointment. I engaged with a travel agency recommended for assisting adoptive families and with the hotel required for at least the first portion of the trip. Having multiple families in one location allows the adoption agency to better assist with logistics of traveling to and from appointments at the orphanage, the administration buildings, and other travel about the city.

We prepared many small gifts for the Thai social workers, caregivers, and others we might encounter on the trip. This is

standard practice for those able to do so and a welcome opportunity to honor those who have cared for your child until you
can bring him or her home. I wrote simple, but heartfelt notes
expressing deep appreciation for their care for our daughter up
to this point. For being the only family she had yet ever known.
These acts of preparation slowly opened the doors of my heart
to feel what was coming, to envision and truly reflect on all the
people who had helped get us and her to this point.

Vince and I decided we would take the boys with us to
Thailand to meet and bring home their sister. The choice was
based on many factors, not the least of which was our belief that
we should become a family unit from the very beginning. Our
daughter was not a baby and would meet her new brothers along
with her parents. I had read many stories and accounts of unifi-
cations and understood that siblings were sometimes helpful in
beginning to navigate the trauma of a child being uprooted from
their home. We were hopeful the boys' presence would help her
feel more comfortable than being with only two adult strangers,
neither of whom looked like her and only one of whom could
speak any Thai.

Another reason for including the boys in the trip was for
the boys themselves. They had been with us since the first adoption efforts and had understood this to be something our family
would do, *as* a family. They didn't complain or question the
decision to adopt and had been gracious and forthcoming in the
home study visits both while overseas and in the U.S. Looking
back, I realize the boys also provided comfort for Vince and me.
These kids already loved us and would be a source of love and
support should our daughter initially reject either or both of us.

Little did we know how critical the choice to bring them along would prove to be.

As the travel dates neared, so, too, did the expiration date of our latest home study. If the Board did not put us on the docket to allow us to travel prior to the expiration, we would have to scramble to complete another home study update. Sure enough, that happened. Once again, I made doctor appointments to document both Vince's and my physical and mental health, requested updated employment verification statements, arranged a visit by a social worker, had the visit, and paid the fee. No matter how close we got, it was clear it was just not going to be real until it was. And as always, we did what needed to be done to keep moving forward.

The boys had each selected a stuffed animal to give their sister when we met her. Quinn had been very attached to his security blanket animal when he was younger, and we wanted to provide their sister every possible source of comfort. We bought clothes of the estimated appropriate size and a mix of engaging toys, balancing anticipated need with mindfulness of not over-packing and knowing we would do some shopping in Thailand. I made arrangements with the boys' teachers to bring along their work and for me to be able to email the teachers for updates and submissions. They were going to miss one week of school and would return with Vince earlier than their sister and I due to U.S. visa processing time in Thailand. With the home study update completed, gifts prepared, and school arrangements made, we were as ready as we could be.

Part Three

CHAPTER 9

Meeting Our Daughter

The trip to Thailand is long. With few exceptions, there are two flights, totaling roughly 18 to 21 hours. If departing from Dulles International Airport, outside of Washington, D.C., the layover is usually either in Seoul, Korea or Narita, Japan. The first time we flew to that region of the world, almost four years prior, we had stopped in Hawaii to visit a friend and relax at the beach before beginning a major transition and life adventure. This trip was different. It was an odd juxtaposition of love and business. Technically, faith in love would be a more accurate description. Can you love someone you've never met? In the case of pregnancy, most people would say yes. In the instance of our attempts to adopt Stephanie, I said yes. In this case, a person of whom we had only seen photos, was it yet love? Or was it a mix of empathy and the hope of love? To truly love someone, you must see them for who they are, accept them as they are, and love them anyway, all the parts of them. We were embarking on the biggest leap of faith in love of our lifetime.

When adopting an 'older' child, their personality is already formed. The whole concept of nature versus nurture comes fully into focus as strangers join to form a family without the adoptive parents having shaped any of the child's habits up to that point. However, behaviors and habits are learned and can be trained. The child has been nurtured to some degree within a completely different culture and scenario. A person's personality and innate preferences are imprinted in their DNA, before any outside force goes to work on 'shaping' them. Most kids grow up wanting to please their parents and do everything they 'should' do.

Parenting is one of life's greatest challenges. Those of us who enter it are all working from whatever experiences we have had in our own lives. Sometimes we default to the patterns of our parents, or we may intentionally work to grow our thinking and evolve into whatever version of parents we seek to become. I believe *most* parents who willfully take on the role go into it with the best intentions and full of love. In every case, each parent carries with them their own history, triumphs, and traumas – some consciously, some tucked away, but still present and influential in their lives.

So, there we were, Vince and I, two imperfect humans, who had already twice become parents and had been learning as we went along, taking the best of our childhoods and trying to become better versions of ourselves as parents. We were enroute to meet a fully formed person, complete with her own personality, no English language ability, no sense of family, but also no existing pressures about who she should be. Certainly, there were routines and norms at The Babies Home in caring for dozens of children. Everyone had to help, but the caregivers did not have their personal egos wrapped up in how any child 'should' be or expectation that a child reflect the caregiver. They were each accepted for who they were and allowed to be themselves within the confines of a safe and sheltered environment and cultural norms. There were no personal belongings and choices were limited. Essentially, our daughter's life, thus far, had been the opposite of what her life was about to become. Two worlds and many hearts were about to collide.

The most affordable flights from the U.S. to Thailand generally arrive in Bangkok late at night. By affordable, I mean right about $1,000 US Dollars per person. Because we were traveling as a party of five, I had prearranged a private shuttle service to our hotel. The use of these services is very common given Thailand's place on travel lists as a top tourist destination. For the most part, you can expect a silver-gray van with cushioned seats, bottled water, and a friendly, professional driver. Our driver was waiting for us with a name placard which was a relief for a tired and anxious family. Surprisingly, I don't have a clear memory of him and didn't take any photos. Anyone who knows me is aware that I take a lot of photos, especially in documenting significant events. This is a learned behavior from my mother, who still does the same.

Early in the adoption process, I had taken photos of almost every person or place that played any role in the progress of the adoption, including the UPS store where we had multiple documents notarized over multiple years. The UPS store and the entire strip mall where it stood has since been demolished and redeveloped, but my memories of going there repeatedly are intact. Other memories, throughout my life, are spotty. They say people won't remember what you said or did, but rather how you made them feel. I believe emotion is what allows us to have a memory imprinted in our hearts and minds and that being fully, consciously present is what allows us to truly feel. By sometimes unconsciously employing behaviors to avoid feeling, i.e., not being fully present, I also inhibited my ability to remember certain times.

Arriving in Thailand, it's possible I had resorted to this pattern, or simply that my mind was swirling. I remember leaving the airport and driving along one of the highways leading into the city. I remember the layout of the hotel lobby and the large hotel room. The hotel had a partnership with the adoption agency and was accustomed to foreign families visiting for the purpose of adoption. The rooms were suite style including kitchens, living areas, and separate bedrooms, which allowed for a comfortable stay with so many people. While somewhat dated, the hotel was spacious and moderately priced. I'm thankful for the photos I took to help me remember the place we first stayed together as a family with our daughter.

Khun Madee, a social worker from the private Thai adoption agency that partnered with the American adoption agency, met us at the hotel along with a van and driver to take us to the orphanage and be with us throughout the day. For the first meeting, we would meet our daughter at the orphanage, go to eat lunch as a group, and then bring her back to the orphanage for what would ultimately be our daughter's final night's stay there. This initial introduction is kind of a litmus test for the Thai social worker and caregivers to observe the interactions. The social worker had seen at least dozens of such unions and presumably all kinds of responses from adoptive parents and children. I don't know what it looks like when it goes poorly, according to their standards, or what exactly would cause them to halt an adoption, but Vince and I were filled with anticipation and some anxiety about how it would go. Our sweet boys, with us every step of the way, provided so much comfort just by being themselves. They each brought the stuffed animal they had selected to give their new sister, a bunny from Boston and a monkey from Quinn. We loaded up into the van and headed to the orphanage.

The Babies Home was a home for newborn babies to children aged up to six years old. It is located about midway between downtown Bangkok and a popular expatriate community. On our trips to Thailand, we had often unknowingly passed by Jessi and the many other children at The Babies Home. Today, we were going to see her first home and meet her for the first time.

We entered the gate and were struck by the beautiful, lush grounds. Tropical weather allows for gorgeous plant life in Thailand. The buildings were small, mostly one-story structures, beige colored with terracotta style roofs. There were street signs pointing to the different buildings and gave it the feel of a small village, which it kind of was. We were taken to a small building with a seating area stocked with books and toys, where we waited. After some time – that felt like forever – but was probably about 20 minutes, the social worker and an orphanage caregiver walked in with our daughter. They had braided her short little curls on both sides, and she wore a lavender Disney princess dress from the communal closet. She was crying and had her head tilted to the side to look away from us. She was tiny and scared and beautiful.

I wanted to rush to her, hold her, and tell her it was going to be okay. Instead, I did the appropriate thing and waited across the room, still practicing the well-developed skills of managing emotions and being patient. The social worker flipped through the pages of the family book we had sent ahead and spoke to Jessi in Thai. She explained who we were and why we were there. At the time, it was not clear whether Jessi had ever seen the book before. Jessi has since told us it was the first time she had seen it, as she stood there, scared, and crying. She had never seen our photos, that she could recall, or been emotionally prepared for this massive change. Boston and Quinn gave their new sister the two stuffed animals. Jessi remembers being shy to accept the toys because she didn't know what they were. She had never seen a stuffed animal.

We all returned to the van to go to lunch. It was awkward. Our daughter sat silent in the van, sometimes looking out the window. During lunch, we chatted with Khun Madee, who was a kind, personable, and sharp professional. She was clearly very experienced in her job. She helped us all to feel more comfortable and provided an opportunity for Jessi to see us simply interacting and as non-threatening. Jessi barely touched her food and could hardly muster a fake smile for a photo. Khun Madee explained they believed Jessi was both scared and excited because she was a curious child. She wanted to know more and was uncertain about the unknown. After lunch, we returned to The Babies Home and said farewell to Jessi for the evening. We all breathed a sigh of relief to have gotten through this first meeting. I'm sure Jessi did too. I wondered if she was hoping we wouldn't return. We had dinner near our hotel at a restaurant called Vincent's, which provided some levity in a very heavy day. None of us remember much about that evening. We were all completely exhausted.

Our initial understanding had been that we would have two days of meetings before bringing Jessi to stay with us. However, we learned the next day that Jessi would come back to the hotel with us that evening. Khun Madee again met us at the hotel, and we returned to the orphanage. I was very interested in documenting all that I could for Jessi about this first part of her life and her first home. The caregivers kindly allowed us to see many areas of the living quarters and talked with us about life at The Babies Home. They entrusted me to take photos for our daughter and not for publication or circulation on social media. I have honored that agreement. The living quarters were simple and clean. There was a large outdoor play area with toys and space to run. There was a bay of bicycles and a spacious dining hall where the children lined up for hand sanitizer before entering to eat. Once again, Jessi barely ate, aware that we were there and shielding her face as she saw me take a couple of photos. I tried to balance the strong desire to document things for her with what, at that point, was the complete intrusion into her life. Our mere presence, having returned for a second day, made it clear that everything she had known up until this point was about to change.

We talked and played with some of the kids. They were especially enthralled with Vince as they did not often see such a large man. The former elementary physical education teacher in him had no problem entertaining and occupying many kids at once. Jessi stood to the side, attentive but not engaged. Knowing her now, I'm certain she was paying attention to every detail despite not outwardly reacting. The boys also played with the kids, once again demonstrating that kindness and laughter are universal languages. It was interesting to see how the other children responded to our presence. They mostly smiled and sought our attention. None of them seemed outwardly confused, having periodically seen Western families arrive and having other friends leave The Babies Home. We took photos of a group of the kids with Jessi and a couple with special friends. One of the caregivers knelt, put her arms around Jessi, offering assurance that all would be okay and telling her that she loved her. The gravity of this moment completely breaks and fills my heart as I think back. That's the dichotomy of adoption. It is equal parts trauma and love. I'm amazed at my ability to stand there holding it together and have shed many tears processing it since.

We went to a small office building to sign paperwork. We presented the many small gifts we had brought for the caregivers and social workers and made a financial donation to The Babies Home. A staff member presented us with a carefully compiled photo album of Jessi's life there, showing her development from infancy to now over five years old. They shared parts of her file with us including baby footprints that I photographed with a pen beside them for reference. Jessi wore an old sundress and plastic flip flops, one of which was missing the tiny rhinestone adornment which was still attached to the other one. The outfit seemed chosen based on items the staff did not mind letting go, knowing Jessi would now have many new clothes of her own. Vince helped Jessi put on a bright pink sweater we had brought for her as the buildings in Thailand can sometimes be overly chilly to balance the sweltering heat outside.

Before leaving the office building, one of the caregivers said, "You're taking one of our best dancers." As a long time dancer, in my younger days, I felt a connection to my daughter in that moment. It didn't matter what kind of dance the caregiver was talking about. Movement is one of life's gifts that brings people together. The Babies Home taught the children Thai dance and would sometimes perform at local festivals. Most recently, prior to our visit, they had taken the children to a nearby beach town to perform Thai dance and enjoy the beach. Our travel had been delayed by one week to allow Jessi this opportunity at the request of The Babies Home. They shared photos from the trip and gave us the 'donation' cup filled with Thai money that audience members had given in support of each dancer. It sits on a shelf in Jessi's room, still full of Thai money and memories.

Prior to departing the grounds of The Babies Home for the last time, we took a family photo that captured the moment. Jessi is crying and not looking at the camera. While she did not physically try to run from the situation, there was a lot of pain inside. We all forced smiles, feeling so many emotions at once. It is difficult to feel happiness or excitement for oneself or family when someone else is clearly hurting, like celebrating a personal achievement amidst a team loss. In the grand scheme of things, our family team was winning; at this moment, though, one team member was in deep distress. Even in times when you believe you are doing something for the greater good, it can be challenging and heartbreaking to get through the moments in between.

Part of the itinerary during adoption trips to Thailand by foreign parents often includes shopping at a local mall. Bangkok has several malls that dwarf American malls and make one wonder who shops at a mall for a Maserati or other luxury goods such as handbags that are heavily marked up due to import taxes. Having visited Thailand so often, I was familiar with the malls and saw little value in such an outing as part of our adoption trip during which time was already very limited. Vince and the boys would return to the U.S. sooner than Jessi and me to minimize time away from work and school while we waited for U.S. visa processing.

We had been told that little was known about Jessi's background. She was found alone and subsequent attempts to locate or determine the identity of her birth parents had been unsuccessful. It is standard procedure in Thailand, when a child is found abandoned, to exhaust all options in trying to identify and locate biological family members. These admirable efforts, with the child's best interests in mind, also delay their eligibility for adoption. The Thai government works to reunite a child with biological relatives, even if not the parents. This is often the goal in the U.S., and likely globally, for the overall wellbeing of the child. It is only after deciding that there is no viable means of family reunification that the Thai government approves for a child to be adopted by another family, sometimes from another country, such as in the case of international adoptions like ours. For all these reasons, I had requested that the Thai adoption agency review Jessi's file once again looking for any information about the area of Bangkok in which she had been found. It is a big city and the part of town where she had been left might hold clues to her background story. Rather than go to a shopping mall, I asked that we be taken to that place, as best it could be determined and located, to document what we could for Jessi and see what I could ascertain. I wanted to take photos and to see, hear, and smell it for myself. I'm so grateful this request was honored as it was one of the most powerful experiences in my entire life.

We were once again in a silver passenger van, the five of us, our Thai adoption agency social worker, and a Thai driver. Khun Madee and the driver communicated back and forth in Thai as we drove through the city. Khun Madee had learned that Jessi was found at a drink stand in a certain part of the city. I don't know exactly what details were available, but it was clear Khun Madee was committed to helping us find the place. As we reached a particular part of the city, Khun Madee directed the driver as she visually scoured the area for clues to identify the spot. We turned onto a side street leading to a parking area between two large buildings that looked like apartments. Rows and rows of windows and balconies with clothes hanging to dry lined each side. We proceeded to the back of the complex where Khun Madee saw people outside and asked the driver to park. Khun Madee and I got out and walked to a courtyard area to speak with someone, while Vince remained in the van with all three kids. As best I could make out, Khun Madee explained the general situation to the man and asked if he could share some information about the area.

The man explained these buildings were Thai government subsidized housing. Most of the residents were from regions outside of Bangkok and came to live and work in the city to make money to send home to their families. Many in this development

were from the south of Thailand, an area about which I had
learned while traveling on vacations in Thailand. The region was
rife with internal conflict over religion and had a culture all its
own. A Muslim insurgency had, for many years now, waged an
ongoing struggle for independence. Roadside improvised explo-
sive devices (IEDs) were common, as were seemingly random
blasts to make their presence known. It was easy to understand
why Thai people from the south would seek a more stable means
for making a living, but not have the resources to do so on their
own. Having learned what we could, Khun Madee and I returned
to the van. I shared some details with Vince as we rode around
the development to take it in. Khun Madee continued to look for
the drink stand.

Ultimately, we made our way back to the main road.
Nearing the point of accepting that we would not be able to locate
the actual place, Khun Madee spotted something and asked the
driver to make a U-turn. As he did so, Khun Madee's eyes were
fixed on what she thought she saw. A drink stand on the side of
the main road, nestled under overgrowth which helped shade it
from the blistering sun. The driver pulled over on the side of the
road and turned on his flashers. Khun Madee and I got out and
walked around the bushes and trees at the entrance and into the
small, covered drink stand. It was a typical Thai convenience
stop with snacks and many colorful drinks. There is a warmth
about these places that transports me mentally to a beachside tiki
stand despite its presence amid city concrete and smog. It was
immediately clear it was the morning and possibly evening stop
for residents of the complex as they set out for or returned from
work for the day. I wasn't sure of its overall operating hours.

Khun Madee approached the woman working behind the counter and greeted her. As they began a conversation, Khun Madee learned the woman was Khun Prisana, the owner of the stand who had been running it for several years. I don't remember if I understood most of the conversation, but Khun Madee translated throughout. She asked Khun Prisana if she remembered finding a baby some years prior. Khun Prisana confirmed that she did remember. Khun Madee asked Khun Prisana to recount whatever she could remember from that day. As Khun Prisana shared what she remembered, and Khun Madee translated, a scenario came into focus for me, which may or may not be even partially accurate, but enabled me to envision what I believe is the most likely situation to have occurred.

I am not a trained psychologist, but I have always been intrigued by the field. My career as an intelligence officer has required that I develop and hone the skill set of reading and understanding people; to ask questions, listen, and withhold judgment. I've learned to assess and seek to understand the motives of people and why they do what they do, not so much in a clinical sense or diagnosis, but more a practical sense. My natural sense of empathy and years of experience assessing human behavior shaped my vision of the story I heard.

Khun Prisana came to work one morning and discovered a baby had been left at her stand. The baby was carefully placed in a box, with a blanket, and covered with mosquito net to protect her. The box was positioned under a small table for added protection, under the cover of the stand itself. Inside the box with the baby was a note, poetically describing the birth date of the baby as, "The third day of the full moon in the twelfth month in the year of the tiger." Khun Prisana alerted the police about the discovery. The baby appeared to be sick, and two policemen took her to a hospital to receive care. She was eventually moved to The Babies Home.

The details provided indicated the level of care taken by whomever placed Jessi at the stand, presumably her birth mother. It is likely the woman was living in the residence, working in the city, away from her home and family in the south. Most Thai people have straight, black hair. Jessi's is curly, which is more common in the south of Thailand. Any guess at the circumstances of the pregnancy or the relationship from which she was born would be mere speculation. However, her birth mother's love was clear. The woman who gave birth to her wanted her to be cared for properly, to be seen and known, as evidenced by providing her date of birth. The woman likely knew what time Khun Prisana came to work each day and probably conversed with her daily as she set out to work. I believe the woman entrusted Khun Prisana to ensure the baby made her way to safety and did all she could herself to protect Jessi until she was found. She may have placed the baby under the table just before dawn, knowing Khun Prisana would soon arrive, and may have even observed from a distance, or perhaps she was too heartbroken to do so.

I have thought about Jessi's birth mother more times than I can count. I was 39 years old when our daughter was born. It's entirely possible that I'm old enough to be this woman's mother too. I care deeply for her. As I watch our daughter grow and develop, I wonder about her. She must be beautiful, sharp, and artistic. She may have a bit of a temper and be strong-willed. I believe she made the choice she needed to for her own survival and for her daughter's. There also exists the possibility that she died giving birth and someone else left the baby. I view this scenario as unlikely. It is befitting of a mother to take the time to poetically write the birthdate the way she did and so lovingly ensure the protection of the child.

As I stood there, listening to the story Khun Madee translated, I could almost feel the presence of our daughter's birthmother. At the same time, I felt myself already becoming her mom. A sense of panic came over me as I wanted to whisk away our daughter quickly because my heart was already attaching and now racing. Logically, though, I reminded myself that, if her birth mother walked up right at that moment and said she wanted to take back her daughter, I would need to let Jessi go. There was a near zero chance that was going to happen and yet the thoughts swirled around in my head. Khun Prisana allowed me to photograph the stand, the table, and herself. I was grateful for the many blessings flowing from this visit.

Khun Madee asked if I wanted her to explain to Khun Prisana who I was. I said "No." She queried if I wanted her to ask any additional questions of Khun Prisana. I took a deep breath, calmed myself, and requested she ask if anyone had ever come back asking about the baby since the day she was left. Khun Prisana said no one had. In that moment, I felt at peace and justified in taking my place as this child's mother. I made an internal promise to fiercely protect her and love her. I was ready to begin it and we left.

When I think about the possible scenarios that led to Jessi being born, it is impossible to know the truth. The story I have accepted as likely may or may not have had her biological father in an active role. We look at life through the filter of our own experiences. My early life did not include my biological father and I think I naturally, even if unfairly, envision or perhaps project a situation where the relationship between Jessi's biological parents was not viable. The possibilities are many in terms of 'who' he was in life, particularly within the context of Thai culture. He might have been a young man also living in subsidized housing and not prepared to accept fatherhood, an older man having an affair with a younger woman, or even an expatriate. Or it may have been the mother who did not want a long-term relationship, for whatever reason. There are countless possible scenarios.

As a woman and as a mother, there are hallmarks of the presence and hand of a woman in the care taken to ensure the baby survived and had a chance. I don't know about her biological father, but I know something about the heart of her biological mother.

An Open Letter to My Daughter's Birth Mother (originally published on www.camoandpearls.net)

Hello.

I think of you from time to time, but especially on Mother's Day. Our daughter is amazing. I am sometimes overwhelmed with gratitude for the opportunity to be her mom, without having endured carrying her in my body. You did that. Thank you for making that choice. Whatever else you may or may not do in your life, you have made the world a better place by blessing it with our girl who is full of light and love.

When I am struck by her beauty, I wonder what you look like. Her eyes are as dark as night and her ebony mermaid hair is gorgeous – although it generally looks like a wild mane in the morning. I continue to learn how to deal with curly hair as it is the complete opposite of mine. You probably know how, and, in time, she will too. She has a tender heart and fierce fighting spirit when she wants to achieve something. Maybe people say the same about you, and I guarantee I will feed both.

Having traveled often in Thailand, experienced the people and culture, and gone to the place she last saw you, I feel like I understand at least the generalities of why you made the next choice, or maybe you felt you had no other choice. Either way, your love for her was evident in the care you took in ensuring she would be safe and that her entry into this world would be known. Thank you for valuing her life and for the gift of documenting her actual birth date, a luxury not afforded to many orphans and adopted children.

Perhaps there were complications. Perhaps the struggle was too great. I know not the nature of the relationship you had with her birth father; human relationships can be so complicated. But it was you who loved her enough to give her life. Please know that I love her enough to give her *a* life, together with the rest of her family and friends. She exhibits many traits that amaze us in their likeness to me. She really is the combination of us both. Nature and nurture, equally important in shaping her identity.

You and I are inextricably linked as mothers to one daughter, and she to both of us. She needs only to look down at her belly button to be reminded of her connection to you and look into my eyes to feel her connection to me. You will forever be in my heart and mind, and I will always speak tenderly about you to our daughter, on Mother's Day, and any time she asks. Without you, there's no her, there's no *us*. Thank you.

Love always,

Holly

CHAPTER 10

Forming a Family in Thailand

Jessi has four parents – two biological parents and two adoptive parents. We share the titles of mother and father, but only Vince and I are 'Mom' and 'Dad'. Jessi's dad has a big, sensitive heart. He freely admits he is the more sensitive of the two of us. While I may be more sentimental and empathetic about many situations, Vince takes things more personally and can be deeply affected by what someone does, or does not, say or do. He is loyal and a fierce protector of all whom he loves. He has been described by many as a big teddy bear, which includes the grumbly, growling part of a bear and the softness of a 'teddy' version. Vince has coached and taught thousands of people from elementary school-aged children to collegiate athletes to adults in the Secret Service. Along the way, he has connected with and cared about many, many people. His head was open to adoption from the beginning, and he finally allowed himself to open his heart to consider how it would feel being a girl dad, something he had always wanted, now possible through adoption. He was ready.

Then, when we took physical custody of Jessi in Thailand, she completely rejected Vince. It was as though he was not in the room. She would not look at him and generally tried to avoid being near him. I was so thankful for the presence of the boys who made Vince feel included and loved every day as we navigated this difficult, initial transition. Outwardly, he kept smiling and supporting me, taking the situation in stride. Inside, I knew it hurt him even as he told himself it would get better. I took opportunities when Vince was playing with the boys to quietly speak to Jessi in Thai, saying "Daddy has a good heart. He will take care of you, too," just as she observed him doing for the boys. Jessi's apprehension was understandable. The children at The Babies Home had little exposure to men and she had possibly never met anyone as big as Vince. His physical stature and presence were unfamiliar to her and likely felt threatening at first, despite having seen him play with other children at The Babies Home. Although she and I were in the nascent phase of building a connection, and I looked nothing like any of her caregivers, I was of a familiar size and gender. She allowed me to physically be near her and care for her.

We traveled to Pattaya, the beach town where we had visited the private orphanage while vacationing in Thailand. Pattaya has an active dark side and a handful of self-contained resorts where a family can stay without really needing to go outside of the confines of the resort. We were visiting the Birds and Bees Resort for the second time. The name initially raises eyebrows, but we had been told about it by an American colleague who had been there with his family. People serving abroad are very good at sharing information with each other to help others experience the best of a region and wider continent and avoid pitfalls they had already encountered.

Birds and Bees is located approximately 90 minutes from Bangkok along the Hu-Kwang Bay. It has an infinity pool, beach area, and a restaurant called Cabbages and Condoms on-site. The restaurant is decorated with artful displays including full-size mannequins and animals made from condoms and supports the cause of community health. The room options vary from standard size to suites to accommodate families and larger groups. We had a second-floor suite overlooking the water and hoped to settle in for a couple of days and begin the process of morphing into a family with a new shape. Much of the clothing we had brought for Jessi was too big, even though we had tried to account for her likely smaller stature. She was almost five and a half years old, but so tiny. Jessi was most comfortable with the boys, often taking their hands to walk between places. They were the calming force for us all and the glue holding us together. They played with Jessi at the beach and made her laugh at the pool. All the while, Vince empathetically allowed space and took some precious videos of this delicate stage. He waited patiently and trusted in what was to come.

Vince's strength and compassion during this time was remarkable and speaks to the man, husband, and father he is. It was he who had dreamed of being a girl parent long before I got my head around it and, here he was, having to sit on the outside watching his new daughter. I continued to reassure Jessi of her daddy. Vince is a man of great faith and it sustained him through this period. I, too, knew that it would not be long before Jessi found in Vince the same security and love that I always had.

One of the most pivotal and stressful parts of the Thailand adoption process is meeting with the Thai Child Adoption Board of the Department of Social Development and Welfare (DSDW). The Department has since changed names to the Department of Children and Youth (DCY). No one departs Thailand with a Thai child without having sat before the Board. The source of anxiety is the concern that they will decide the family is not a good fit for a child. I don't know how often this occurs, but the sheer prospect of it – after years and years of process and commitment, waiting, and prayer – is terrifying. The entire adoption trip is scheduled based around the family's assigned board meeting. Potential adoptive parents correspond regularly and support each other via private social media groups. The annual list of board meetings for the coming year is always a hot topic because everyone knows that, if they get to travel to bring home their child, it will be based around one of those dates.

It was now our turn. We traveled together to the administrative office building that housed DSDW and hosted the Board meetings. We waited our turn and briefly saw our Thai government social worker, Khun Achara – the same one with whom I'd met while we were living in Southeast Asia and with whom I had corresponded after returning home. I presume she explained to Jessi what was going to happen. Jessi did not look happy and was quiet as we waited. She probably felt comfortable back in the presence of the Thai social worker and so many other Thai people but may have also been reminded we would not be staying in Thailand.

When we entered the room to meet with the Board, it felt a bit like a court room, not so much because of how it looked but because of the deliberative nature of the exchange. We were asked some questions relating to our intent to care for Jessi. We answered sincerely and expressed our appreciation for the opportunity to adopt a Thai child. Respect is very important within Thai culture and is one of our family's primary values. Our gratitude was and is genuine. The Board approved the continuation of the process and allowed us to take legal custody of Jessi. When it was time to depart, we took photos in front of the entrance to the Child Adoption Center.

This began a six-month probationary period during which we would have bimonthly visits by a social worker in the U.S. to observe our family in our home and see firsthand the progress of the transition. On this day, however, we were excited to be one step further in the process. Anxious, nervous, full of hope, and holding onto faith.

In this short time together, Jessi had rapidly attached to her brothers. The void left by the loss of all her orphanage friends and family was awkwardly, partially filled by these two Western boys who were five and six years older than her. They were more like her than her new mom and dad and she trusted them implicitly. Unfortunately, we had to stick with our prearranged travel plans that had Vince and the boys departing first. In hindsight, I would probably have planned differently, as it began one of the hardest weeks ever for Jessi and me.

On the final day that Vince and the boys were in Thailand, we were in the hotel room passing time until they departed for the airport. In this quiet time, Jessi had a breakthrough moment with Vince. It seemed she was starting to open her heart and mind to him as they played together, and I took the first photo we had of the two of them smiling together. Knowing my child so well now, it was a genuine smile unlike many of the forced ones she gave while soldiering through this transition. Then, the guys had to leave, and the ensuing firestorm took us all by surprise.

As we hugged to say farewell, Jessi realized what was happening but could not comprehend the context and temporary nature of the separation amidst a language barrier and ongoing trauma. The two people who had quickly become her lifeline through loss, and the third whom she was finally beginning to trust, were now leaving. More loss. When Vince and the boys walked out of the hotel room door, Jessi broke. She ran after them, screaming and crying. I chased her to the door, and she made it out before I could get to her. I don't remember how I kept us from being locked out of the room. I looked up and saw our three guys at the elevator with their suitcases, not looking back because they knew they had to keep going. I struggled to get Jessi back into the hotel room where we spent the afternoon together in crisis.

That evening, when it was time for bed, we were both very much in need of sleep. The mental and emotional toll left us exhausted. When I guided Jessi to bed, she began crying and repeating in Thai, "Kidtung phii," which translates to 'I miss my brothers.' It was a brokenhearted, drawn out, wailing tone that I would hear every night for the next week, at least fifty times each night, inconsolable. I tried to ease the pain through preemptive distraction, reading books and pointing to the pictures. But I knew what was coming as soon as we finished the book each night. She would cry for her new brothers who had left. For her 'brothers' and 'sisters' whom she had left at The Babies Home. For her new father whom she had just met and was now gone. She would cry and cry, saying "I miss my brothers," until she could no longer get out the words. And finally, she would sleep. Until the next morning when we would begin again.

CHAPTER 11

The Longest Week

The next week was a bit of a blur as Jessi and I trudged through each day, with Jessi not knowing or fully understanding why her new family had left while she and I were still in Thailand. Ice cream became my go-to for providing Jessi some temporary relief from the Bangkok heat, and distraction from the turmoil she was experiencing. We explored the city together. I revisited many places I was familiar with from traveling and Jessi saw several for the first time. We were two strangers, spending every day and night together, not yet truly connected, clinging to and resisting each other simultaneously.

With all the guys gone, Jessi directed all her pain at me. I stood alone in my faith to face the wrath that came out of this child each time something triggered her, and she was unable to keep it in. At times, I was terrified. Scared of what she might do and what I might need to do to try to control her. Scared that hotel staffers or other patrons would hear the screams and think I was hurting her. I was on eggshells every day. Worried that she would have an outburst while we were out having lunch or visiting a culturally important place. Yet, the thought of staying in the hotel room was equally stress-inducing as she was more likely to have a tantrum there. Before meeting Jessi, I had read the little information made available about her. I remembered a line in the report that said, when she was upset or did not get her way, verbatim (including the grammatical error), "She may cries and scream a lot." When I read it, I assumed it referred to a typical toddler outburst, and was not overly concerned. My frame of reference was my own life experience and I had never witnessed the level of emotion from a child that Jessi would later display.

As we moved through that long week together, we visited several icons of Thai culture and Thai life. I took photos of Jessi at the Grand Palace, the BTS (sky train), and eating ice cream, pretty much everywhere we went. I felt it was important to document that she, as a Thai person, had visited some of these places before leaving her birth country. I took photos from both front and rear views as we were not allowed to publish her face on social media or anywhere until the adoption was finalized. I envisioned her one day returning at an age and time when she would be able to remember the experience and recognize the value to her Thai identity of having physically been there as a Thai child.

We rode in tuk-tuks many times. Tuk-tuks are small, three-wheeled motorized vehicles that seat anywhere from two to four people comfortably. There is no set fee, and you generally negotiate up front to avoid the driver asking an exorbitant rate once you've reached your destination, and you feel obliged to pay it. For an average ride between two downtown locations, 100 Thai baht (~$3) is reasonable. If you're not savvy, you may find a driver pushing for up to 500 Thai baht (~$17). Having lived at The Babies Home, as far as we know, Jessi never had the opportunity to ride in a tuk-tuk. It became one of her favorite things to do. She loved to *go*. Anything with motion or movement, or new experiences, she was up for. Even things that caused her to feel fear. It is the element of her personality that both helped her to be resilient in the face of change and trauma and to fight to protect herself until she learned that she didn't need to do so with her new family.

During our week alone in Thailand, Jessi experienced many 'firsts,' including getting her first pair of shoes, at five and a half years old. For the most part, kids at The Babies Home wore flip flops and sandals from a shared supply. Jessi rode the sky train for the first time and went to local stores. A family fishing trip in the week prior had also been a first. So many firsts, all special, all impactful, and only the beginning of the 'firsts' that would happen as she became part of our family.

When I hear people talk about 'firsts', my perspective is based upon having both biological children and an adopted child. I don't remember several of the boys' firsts – first words, etc. I remember when Boston started walking independently only because it was the night before we went to the hospital for Quinn's caesarean delivery. The thought of two children not yet able to walk seemed slightly overwhelming. (Shout out to parents of twins!) I distinctly remember Vince walking out the front door, holding Boston's hand, on the way to his parents' house where Boston would stay for the night. It was an answered prayer to see our little guy walking on his own. Other than that, most of the others are a blur.

With Jessi, I always view it from a place of gratitude *that* she walks and *that* she talks. Not having been present for Jessi's first step or first Thai word is irrelevant because I can't get those times back, and I have her in front of me now. I can be present for the firsts that matter to her.

During our remaining stay in Bangkok, Jessi and I met for dinner with several of my Thai friends. They had known Vince and I were in the process of adopting a Thai child and, like most other Thai people, found it somewhat perplexing. Thai people are generally very kind *and* direct. It is an interesting juxtaposition as they will ask questions that, from a fellow American, would seem rude, but put in the context of Thai culture were not. This is not to say there is no judgment in Thai culture. There definitely is. They just work harder to make people feel comfortable rather than projecting their judgment. Nonetheless, dinner was uncomfortable in hindsight, a terrible idea from the standpoint of Jessi's situation and feelings. While I wanted to share the wonderful news with my Thai friends, I didn't truly consider Jessi's feelings. My ego subconsciously drove the desire to show that determination pays off. This is one of the perils of being a driven, competitive person, and a byproduct of the emotional-clinical tug of war that occurs internally throughout the adoption process.

If Jessi could have disappeared from dinner, I have no doubt she would have. She sat slumped and silent the entire time. There was zero validation or evidence that this was a good thing and I suspect my Thai friends felt conflicted in seeing one of their own in such a state. Fortunately, I have since had the opportunity to share with one of them how Jessi is thriving now. In that moment, though, I felt ashamed, certainly not of Jessi or of adoption, but of myself for making the choice to put her through this evening.

When it was finally time to visit the U.S. Embassy to receive Jessi's U.S. visa, I was excited to be that much closer to going home; not because I don't love Thailand, but because I would be returning to the love and support of family and friends. I say 'I' instead of 'we' because Jessi did not have that same comfort. A surprise was the brief relief I felt by being in the presence of other Americans. U.S. State Department Consular Officers who see adoptive families in many countries throughout the world and have the perspective of life in America versus life in other countries. In this space, I was not judged, and my motives were not ambiguous or questioned. These fellow patriots knew what I knew: That despite all our faults, the United States of America remains a beacon of hope and a light for the world. Our freedoms are unparalleled, and our hearts are big. In Thailand, the most serious crime is speaking against the monarchy which, to be clear, I am not doing here. In the U.S., people verbally disparage leadership every day and their right to do so is protected. The power and, in comparison to many countries, uniqueness of that freedom is sometimes lost on the free and privileged.

At the embassy, I was reminded that this adoption *was* a good thing and that all the struggle was going to be worth it.

For family, for freedom, and for the opportunity for my child to become all that she is meant to be, whatever she decides that is.

I was ready when it was time to go to the airport. I worried about how the trip might go and prayed Jessi would stay calm. On our way to the international departures terminal, we were required to stop to meet with a Thai immigration official. Khun Madee had provided us with documents to present upon departure which explained the scenario. This is a critical vetting procedure given the prevalence of human trafficking of children worldwide. I handed our travel documents and the letter to the uniformed Thai officer. He carefully read them and looked them over extensively. He looked up at me and then at Jessi. She did not look happy but sat silent. I sensed the officer felt the same mixed feelings my Thai friends had. It was a heavy moment where I felt, for a second, like he might refuse our departure. Again, I also felt shame for 'taking' something, someone, whom they perceived as not mine to take. It's possible they, too, feel some shame for not caring for their own. Neither of us should feel shame for the situation but it is a complex scenario and human nature is what it is. The official handed us back our documents and allowed us to proceed.

We made our way to the terminal and found seats in the waiting area. As we sat down, I was overcome by the weight of taking a child from her birth country. It was so tangible that I could barely contain my emotions. I told myself I could not cry because Jessi would not understand. I needed to be strong for her. Having traveled often in Thailand, I knew firsthand the sights, the sounds, and the smells of this amazing country that had been her home and would always be her birthplace. This was the flip side of what I felt at the embassy. There were once again coexisting and somewhat conflicting truths. I was taking her to an amazing country to become part of a loving family and provide her with all that we could. I was also taking *from* her all that she had ever known, and it ripped me apart inside. As I felt my eyes begin to well up with tears, I forced the emotion down and outwardly held myself together. I made a promise to myself to keep her Thai identity and heritage alive and well. That we, as a family, provide opportunities for her to live it, for all of us to celebrate it, and for her to always be proud of the beautiful country that made her and lives in her.

The flight was relatively uneventful with only a few struggles including the need to wear a seatbelt. We made it safely to the U.S. and deplaned. Vince and I had decided to keep things both simple and normal, so the guys were not at the airport when we arrived. It was somewhat anticlimactic; but the last thing Jessi needed was a dramatic display or production upon her arrival. Hindsight being 20/20, I could really have used the support and relief, and she would probably have been thrilled to immediately see her brothers. As it was, we got someone to snap a photo, I used an app to get us a ride, and off we went. I felt comfort, relief, and anticipation to get back to our house. Jessi felt none of that as evidenced by her stoicism in the photo we took. From this point forward, everything she saw and heard would be new to her. She was now on the other side of the world and, while she didn't understand that, I know everything felt different. She couldn't understand a single word being spoken around her and nothing smelled the same.

When we arrived at the house, I took a photo of her walking up the sidewalk for the first time. Inside, my mother had neatly arranged toys for Jessi in the recreation room and her bedroom was beautifully prepared, just as I had left it. I can only imagine the thoughts and emotions swirling around in Jessi's head as she halfheartedly played with some of the toys and explored the house. Like the night in Thailand between meeting Jessi and taking custody of her, no one in the family can remember anything else about the moment or evening we were all reunited as a family.

Early the next morning, before it was time to get up, I woke up to use the bathroom. As I walked past the door to our bedroom, I saw Jessi standing quietly in front of her bedroom door. Imagine her confusion waking up in a strange place and remembering she had traveled far from home. For over five years, she had slept on the floor in a room with the many children who were her family. Now, she was in a bed alone in a room she did not recognize in a house with people she did not yet really know. She may have even gotten up to use the bathroom herself and felt unsure where to go. At The Babies Home, the caregivers on duty would go around in the middle of the night, waking the children to use the restroom by snapping a towel, presumably so as not to have to bend over to reach each child. Jessi has since recounted that memory multiple times because it annoyed her so much. She has also shared, however, that the children had rotating opportunities to sleep in a bed with the caregiver on duty for the night to feel the love of a mother and the comfort of a proper bed.

Standing in the hallway landing area, Jessi looked so tiny. She *was* so tiny. It was in these moments, these spaces between tantrums and moods, that I could feel genuine empathy and love for my new child. I calmly approached Jessi and guided her downstairs and offered something to eat. And so began a massive life shift for our family and five difficult months.

CHAPTER 12

Trauma and Transition

The physical recovery of childbirth, for me, even recovering once from an episiotomy and once from a C-section with a fractured tailbone, paled in comparison to this situation – leading and navigating myself, a new child, my husband, two biological children, friends, and family through the trauma and transition of adoption of a child who could not even communicate her thoughts and feelings in the language by which she was now surrounded. While we had been required to attend hours and hours of training, in Thailand and in the U.S., online and in-person, nothing had prepared me or any of us for what we would experience over these months. I later wondered why. Was it assumed that, if you had biological children, you had experienced tantrums of this magnitude? Or are tantrums of this level not that common? Was there a fear that brutal honesty might scare away potential adoptive parents? Possibly neither of these things is the case and the training simply keeps the focus on understanding the trauma that adoptive children face. However, there is no positive situation that results in a child being without one or both of their biological parents. There is always loss. The body and soul feel and know it well before the brain and heart can process it. More thorough discussions, during adoption training, of how this pain may manifest itself in behavior would be beneficial for the child to better allow adoptive parents to prepare and ultimately support the child and cope themselves.

The morning after we returned from Thailand, I took Jessi to kindergarten orientation. She was jetlagged, unable to understand English, and not yet in a place where I could provide real comfort to her. On the positive side, it may have been a slight relief to see so many other children, like at The Babies Home, but not the same. Jessi met her teacher, Marcia. Jessi was instantly drawn to Marcia's warmth and the attention she gave to all the children. I think Marcia's classroom felt the most like home of anything Jessi experienced during her move to the U.S. Unable, yet, to speak English, Jessi called her 'Missuh Moonyo', the closest she could get to annunciating her actual name.

I had known Marcia for several years through our oldest sons who had been classmates and friends. She was fully aware of our adoption process, and I had prayed (and possibly lobbied) to get her assigned as Jessi's teacher. I was grateful to receive the news that she was. I trusted Marcia to be attentive to Jessi's needs and to work with us in meeting them, while not paying more attention to Jessi than the other kids. As I think back, I realize I trusted her to also meet *my* need for communication outside the classroom. Jessi's acclimation process was going to require a true partnership. Like Jessi, I, too, was in such a fragile place that my expectations of support were unusually high. With three children of her own, an entire classroom of kids just beginning school, and concurrently being the kindergarten team lead, Marcia met this challenge with grace, professionalism, and empathy.

During the orientation, I left Jessi in the classroom with the other kids for the designated amount of time. This section of orientation was designed to help the kids, and parents, get used to having the children be in a classroom independently, which was new for many. I felt anxious and scared about how Jessi would do in my absence, not yet realizing the temper tantrums were released only in my presence. Later, Marcia offered reassurance that Jessi had done fine, and it would all be okay. We just had to get through the next four months until school actually started.

In the coming year, Marcia built a loving and nurturing relationship with Jessi, not different than the way she supports all her students, but certainly making Jessi feel special and cared for. Although she was 15 years into her career, at this point, it *was* a unique scenario for Marcia in her teaching career. Marcia consistently reminded me that Jessi's progress was remarkable given the starting point. By the end of the school year, Jessi was reading on grade level, in the second language she had learned before the age of six. Marcia's contributions to Jessi's development were instrumental. The balance of instruction and care allowed Jessi to thrive in this foreign environment. Marcia has impacted the lives of hundreds of children over the years and her dedication to all of them is to be applauded. But, for us, it is her unwavering support for our adopted child that evokes deep, eternal gratitude for being a pillar of love, hope, and opportunity for all. Marcia has said "Jessi is a special one. She changed me.

I'm a better teacher because of what she taught me." Thank you, Marcia. We love you.

I had taken off work for the adoption travel and an extended time after. At that time, in the U.S. government (USG), there was still no use of medical leave allowed for transition after adoption. No paid parental leave was granted for childbirth either. I'm thankful this has since changed for all parents who work for the USG. I had saved enough annual leave to split the time out of the office between annual leave and leave without pay, reducing my salary by half. It added additional strain but was a necessary step to get us through this time. The boys had another six weeks of school and Vince was working full-time. We could not afford to have both of us take off without any paid parental leave. So, each morning, the three guys got up to go to work and school and Jessi and I were home. Here, we found ourselves alone, together again. Jessi was dealing with the significant loss and confusion about her new situation. I was desperately in need of some decompression and processing time that was not coming anytime soon.

I felt the weight of two monumental and critical tasks, although one was of greater significance than the other. One was to help her learn English. The other was to help her feel safe and loved. Getting to the place of understanding family was a loftier goal and longer-term aspiration. I was not a trained educator. I had coached primarily high school aged kids for many years, but as any career educator or developmental psychologist will tell you, each age of development requires different ways of teaching.

I filled the days with a mix of educational activities, including workbooks and computer games, and play. Jessi was initially only moderately interested in English language TV. We knew *Tom & Jerry* had been a favorite at The Babies Home. The cartoon has no spoken language and Jessi could simply follow along and relax a bit. She would work diligently on worksheets before even understanding the new alphabet in front of her. It allowed a sense of accomplishment which always seemed important to her along with the praise that came after.

When it came to play, Jessi and I both struggled, while it came naturally to her dad and her brothers. Through therapy in processing my own childhood, I discovered I had sometimes felt like I needed to be more mature than my years based on various life experiences and circumstances. I have a well-developed sense of humor and quick wit, but I am not a particularly playful person outside of athletics or humor. Play is important for people of all ages, so I have worked to get better at allowing myself that space, partly beginning during this time with Jessi. I don't spend time daydreaming, but I do have great vision and believe in purposeful visualization of goals and ideas. Making things happen is a challenge I enjoy. Turning visions from imagination to reality is amazing. So, I started there with Jessi.

Jessi's life experience prior to being in our family was so limited that there wasn't much to draw from in terms of imagination and creativity. Add to that the language barrier and we found ourselves in a real predicament. I was thinking to myself "Okay, how do I do this?" and Jessi was looking at me thinking "Okay, what do we do now?" There was a lot of staring. Without other kids around and no understanding of this new world, she was completely dependent on me to guide her. It seemed we each had a feeling of having a spotlight on us in a way neither of us ever had before.

One day we sat on the floor to build with blocks. Jessi did the only thing she knew or could think of and stacked them one on top of the other until they fell. My teaching skills were really being tested and her development cycle was years behind a child who grew up in a home from birth. I used an iPad to pull up pictures of things and then did my best to replicate them with blocks. A space shuttle, a giraffe, and so on. I don't know if she even had any idea what the pictures were, but she began to see the association between looking at something and then making it ourselves. The process couldn't fill her mind with knowledge of things she had not yet seen, but it did spark the concept of possibility and the beginnings of creativity. Her building became more diverse, not really looking like any discernible object, but differing shapes well beyond that initial straight, tall tower of blocks. Witnessing each small glimpse of progress and seeing them as positive was critical for us both. It allowed me to see tangible evidence that I was helping her and, as I praised her efforts, she felt a sense of achievement. Meanwhile, we were bonding through our efforts to play, and it gradually became more natural.

Another example of Jessi's unfamiliarity with basic concepts for American children and undeveloped imagination came during her first bath. At The Babies' Home, the kids had all showered together, divided by gender, in a locker room style setup. Jessi now found herself in a room where people usually went individually to use the toilet or the shower. This was a foreign concept for her to begin with. As the boys and I excitedly filled the bathtub with warm water, practically overflowing with soap suds, we carefully helped Jessi get into the tub. At that point, she kind of looked at us as if to say, "What do I do now?" Boston was on his knees beside the tub, demonstrating how to play with toys and making funny sounds. Quinn put some suds on her head, and we all laughed. Even with the group effort to entertain Jessi, she seemed bored with the whole thing. It didn't last long, and I don't remember if we ever did it again. But I did capture one of my favorite pictures of the three of them from those early days.

While traveling in Thailand, my Thai language skills had not proven to be quite good enough to order a cell phone in a Thai mall without the entire staff gathering around to watch and listen. Regardless, it turned out all those night classes after work had been time well spent, after all, so that I could communicate with Jessi on a kindergarten level. With no exaggeration, she did not speak a single word of English when we met her. She was now experiencing full immersion language training.

Before leaving Thailand with Jessi, I recorded a video of her 'reading' a book in Thai. While she couldn't read the English words, she looked at the illustrations and narrated the story. I was able to understand her Thai interpretation. This is the only video we have of Jessi speaking fluent Thai, complete with tonal intonations, and it is a blessing of immeasurable value. It marks a time to which we cannot return, when she spoke Thai from birth, and had not yet learned English.

I had read that there was no need to say both the native tongue and English words while pointing to an object, but I used Thai language more for basic concepts that were not specific items to which I could point. We used ABCmouse.com and Jessi very much enjoyed the animations as she got the hang of using the computer and mouse. I often gave her some space in hopes she would feel more comfortable repeating the words without me standing over her. Although there were some moments when it seemed she wanted me to see how hard she was trying, and I was sure to provide praise.

As Jessi learned English, she rapidly forgot Thai, and it was heartbreaking to witness this loss of part of her birth identity and hallmark of her ethnicity. We knew it was critical that she become fluent in English, but I wished I was able to speak enough Thai to do so exclusively with her at home. One day, I said something to her in Thai and she responded in English, "That's very good, Mom." She could understand what I said although she probably would have struggled to find the Thai words herself, at that point. It was as though she had forgotten I had spoken only Thai to her in the early days. I knew in that moment that I had to let it go, for the time being, and hoped we would one day return to Thai language together.

Because I have a basic understanding of Thai grammar, I was able to understand Jessi's juxtaposition of words in sentence structure. This allowed me to help her work through learning more complex English grammar. In Thai, there is no conjugation of verbs, and qualifiers come after the verb. For example, 'I run yesterday. I run today.' Additionally, adjectives follow a noun, so, 'two smart boys' would be translated in Thai as 'boy smart two person'. Because words are made plural by stating how many rather than by adding an 's' as in English, Jessi would always drop the 's'. We made a game of it such that, when it occurred, I would ask something like "Just one arm?" and she would respond "Two arm-*sss*" with an extra emphasis on the 's'.

When Jessi entered school in the U.S., she was enrolled in an enrichment class for English Speakers of Other Languages (ESOL) as part of her curriculum. The majority of other ESOL students were native Spanish speakers. Because the instruction was in English with a focus on English language rather than translation from a native language, the difference did not hinder Jessi's progress. By the end of her kindergarten year, Jessi was reading on grade level in English and has done so ever since. She is an avid reader which has enabled her to maintain this remarkable achievement.

I feel strongly about providing Jessi the opportunity to relearn Thai language to remain deeply connected to her Thai heritage. If she chooses to pursue multiple languages, we will support her in that endeavor as well. However, I struggle to find the logic in requiring her to learn a third language in her life without relearning her birth language. Jessi has already experienced full immersion language training, so the idea of familiarization with a 'second' language does not hold weight. Nonetheless, absent any evidence that learning a third language is detrimental to her development, and is probably positive overall, it has been easier, thus far, to allow her to follow along with her peers for social development.

I envision Jessi and I pursuing Thai language classes together and one day being able to communicate in Thai without those around us being able to understand – our own private way to communicate as we did in the early days of the adoption. However, Vince has expressed an interest in resuming Thai lessons as well. I suppose a family communication language would be just as special and fun as sharing a secret code. Sort of.

Most days, there was at least one major tantrum, almost always when we were home alone, and one in the car leaving a school function we had attended for the boys. I existed in a constant state of anxiety, which I realize is a word used multiple times in this book, regarding when the next tantrum would occur and what would be the trigger. They had become more dramatic and intense including the same stomping and screaming, but now including sometimes breaking things and hurting herself or me. Jessi would sometimes compulsively dig her fingernails into her legs, causing them to bleed, or chase me around the house to hit me as I tried to give some space to the situation. She wanted me 'in it' with her, no matter how badly I wanted out. She seemed to be seeking physical release of the internal pain. She remained in significant trauma, and I was traumatized as well.

Each day, when the boys and Vince came home, she was all smiles for them. They continued to be loving and supportive to us both, as one would hope. However, I began to resent that I was going through hell every day only to have everyone else experience all the desired joys. I shared with Vince that this arrangement was not working for me. He immediately said, "Just tell me what you want me to do. What do you need?" I said I needed him to demonstrate to Jessi that her behavior toward me was not okay. In learning about family, even amidst grief, she needed to learn that we were a team. She would then learn that she did not have to choose between us, nor was it allowable to lash out at Mom all day when no one was around and then have the entire family behave as though nothing happened.

There is no manual for every parenting situation, be it a biological child or an adoptive child. Much of the available literature I found suggested giving a lot of latitude in behaviors during transition in adoption. We felt, however, the longer we allowed it to continue unchecked, the more normal it could become as I grew further away in navigating my own trauma and resentment. Logic does not always prevail when you are in pain. While far from perfect parents, we had raised our boys, thus far, with a significant amount of structure and clear boundaries that had helped shape them into respectful children. Vince and I decided together to go back to what we knew and add in certain modifications based on the uniqueness of adoption. We utilized 'time in' instead of 'time out'. The idea is, rather than send the child away to their room or somewhere else alone, and away from the family to which you want them to bond, address the behavior and have them sit for a certain time, in one spot in the same room with a parent or the family, whomever is around. This did not work, however, when Jessi and I were home alone. She would simply get up and follow me. However, having Vince come home and calmly tell her it was not okay to hit Mommy or throw things then have her sit on the sofa for 'time in,' when he was nearby in his chair, had an impact.

When Jessi would begin a tantrum during the day, I would say I was going to call Daddy, to which she would respond "No, no," and settle down. She had already grown to love her dad's hugs and play time and did not want to disappoint him. It's possible that counselors and psychologists would explain some potentially harmful effects of some aspect of how we handled things, but we were surviving and were not using physical punishment. This was progress for each of us given our childhoods had different boundaries and forms of discipline. Gradually, as the days went on and we all moved forward in adapting, the tantrums slowly decreased, but they continued periodically for a while longer.

Sometimes, just before a tantrum, Jessi's facial expression would visibly change. Her eyes narrowed and she stared straight ahead. Instantly, my blood pressure rose as I had yet to discover a way to calm the chaos before it began. One day, still amid near daily, very dramatic tantrums, was uniquely memorable. After a battle over some boundary, I had calmly taken away one of Jessi's toys. As she stood at the top of the landing of the split-level stairs, I saw the dark mood wash over her. She started slowly stomping her feet in protest, lifting, and putting down one, then the other, and repeating. It felt like an eerie build up to an eruption, and it was.

Much of the tantrum is blank in my mind and I next remember us sitting on the couch, side by side, not touching each other, as she continued screaming and crying. She repeatedly yelled in Thai "I don't want to watch this!" about whatever was on TV. I was shaking and rattled to my core, and I started praying out loud. The more I prayed, the angrier she got. Despite not yet speaking fluent English, she turned and looked directly at me and began screaming, "Stop it! Stop it!" Her voice had a low, gravely tone and the English was perfectly clear. It was chilling. I was shocked as I turned to stare into her eyes, and I didn't feel like I was looking at my child. I prayed louder as the battle raged and was now confident because I know how to fight this enemy. Eventually, calm returned as I found myself sitting beside my daughter again. She allowed me to hug her as we both recovered.

Each night, going forward, when she would go to bed, after she had fallen asleep, I would go into her room, lay hands on her, and pray. It was yet another form of advocacy for my child. In keeping with my belief system, I was putting Satan on notice that he would not consume my daughter, a child of God, regardless of origin, and that I was prepared to continue to fight for her every single day. The frequency of tantrums which had decreased some, now rapidly decreased. No matter what your belief system, anyone who had been in the room and witnessed it would have become a believer in something other than the visible. It was unreal. Except it *was* real.

Prior to bringing Jessi home, we had been gifted several bags of clothing for Jessi from a family with two daughters and a son who was a classmate and friend of Boston's. They passed us the clothing through another family friend. I was excited as I looked through the beautiful clothes and asked again about the family who sent them. I couldn't remember having previously met Heather, the mother who had so generously gone out of her way to extend this kind gesture, although I may have met her through youth football. I sent a thank you note to express our gratitude.

When I had the opportunity to meet Heather at the elementary school, I thanked her again and shared with her how things were going. Heather is a preschool special education teacher and well-versed in dealing with a wide range of behavioral issues. She is also a loving wife and mom and one of the most genuine people I've ever met. I felt immediately comfortable sharing our struggles with her. It wasn't something just anyone was prepared or interested to hear. Most people envisioned an idyllic scenario in which Jessi was so happy to be out of an orphanage and living with a loving family – an overly simplistic expectation of a situation that can only truly be understood by living or studying it, which is partially why I'm sharing.

Each time I saw Heather, she listened empathetically and, just as importantly, shared tactical advice on managing tantrums. She coached me on how to safely restrain your child so that they neither hurt themselves nor their parent or caregiver. This was not something I had ever previously had to do, but I now found myself a student of practical maneuvers to manage behavior born from emotional trauma. These unexpected conversations empowered me and let me know I wasn't alone in having to deal with violent tantrums. I now had skills to help myself and Jessi get through these times and a friend to whom I could speak about it without fear of judgment.

My love and respect for Heather runs deep because of her giving of herself and her knowledge during this very difficult period. While our sons were first friends, our youngest children later became teammates and friends, too. I'm so grateful that God placed Heather in our lives when he did and I'm proud to call her my friend, still. Thank you, Heather.

One of the biggest challenges was imposing structure. While one might assume there was significant structure in a group home, routines are not the same thing as structure. Certainly, they can go hand in hand, but one does not guarantee the other. The days and nights at The Babies Home had routines, set times to do certain things. In the spaces between, however, there was a lot of free play, mostly outside, with limited choices of what to do. So, now, Jessi found herself in a place with many more choices and many more rules. It was very often confusing and frustrating for her. It was critical, though, that she learn these things within the home to get to a place where she could be without us outside of the home, such as school in a few months.

When the boys finished school for the year, summer break allowed an opportunity for Jessi to see daily that structure and boundaries applied to everyone, not just her. She saw her brothers repeatedly corrected and still loved. She saw them eat their veggies and be excused from the table while she sat and stared at hers. This is another example where parents may disagree on how to handle it or assess it as not a battle worth fighting, but for us, consistency was critical. We had always stayed the course with the boys and the results spoke for themselves in terms of their behavior, even if exhausting for Vince and me along the way.

'Parent' is both a noun and a verb and we were committed to the *act* of parenting in addition to being parents. While the adoption scenario was different than with our prior kids, we opted to calmly hold to the core principles of accountability. Every family must make their own choices based on their own children.

In addition to new choices, Jessi now had personal belongings, something she had never experienced before. Early after arrival in the U.S., I once commented that there were a lot of things on her dresser and, before I could say I wanted to straighten up, she said with a smile, "Yes, and they're mine," in Thai. In that moment, I realized the importance of having her own things in her new home. It was now clear why, every day, multiple times a day, she would pick up something and ask "Khong khrai?" Who does this belong to? It mattered to her. Most kids need to learn to share. Jessi needed to first learn to *possess* and how to handle it. Sharing becomes less attractive once you understand something belongs to you. "Khong chan." It belongs to me.

In Thai culture, there is an emphasis on appearances and presentation. Making things and people look nice and feel comfortable is important. This is not a negative generalization as there are many positive elements to this trait, from beautiful displays and fun marketing campaigns to towels folded into the shape of a heart or a dove with flowers when you check into a resort. There is a certain pride of ownership and desire for harmony that fits in with the overall nature of the Land of Smiles. Of course, this does not apply to every person, all the time. When it comes to children, however, it's very common to highlight that a little girl is 'Suaj maak,' very pretty, or even in English, 'So cute.' This habit, combined with a youthful tendency to raise the pitch of one's voice and pose, or comment on something or someone as 'cute,' quickly seeps into the psyche of a child.

Jessi came to us already adept at putting on appearances. She was in turmoil inside but knew how to put on the act of happiness to garner praise from those around her. I don't have any knowledge or information regarding how often compliments were given at The Babies Home for anything other than appearance. I also never had the opportunity to observe a Thai classroom. However, I imagine that, in the context of a group home, there is some emphasis on building a child's self-esteem, including appearance.

Initially, we were limiting how much time we spent outside of the house meeting new people. It's called cocooning and is a recommended practice during adoption transitions for allowing the new family to build connections. As a family, we would go to the boys' sporting events, and I would periodically take Jessi to the store with me. It was a lot for her to take in. Moving about amongst strangers was less of an issue because they were unaware of the scenario taking place in front of them and went about their business. Acquaintances, however, knowing we were adopting a child, were often curious to see her in real life. With few exceptions, people would almost immediately comment on her appearance, with good intent and not knowing we were trying to address this issue. It was so pervasive that I would either try to interrupt before people could get out the words or even drag my finger across my lips or neck to signal not to continue. I have

no doubt that my behavior was sometimes puzzling to others
and may have seemed harsh, none of which mattered to me or
us, as we worked to build new, healthy pathways of development
for our daughter.

At The Babies Home, their primary job was to keep the
kids healthy and cared for, which they did. Jessi had five years of
programming that may or may not have included any focus on
being smart, strong, or brave. I don't know. Anyone who knows
me knows that I care deeply about helping kids believe in themselves much sooner in life than I did. With my daughter, I was
working against already formed patterns and beliefs. But I have
never interpreted difficult to mean impossible. I was determined
and I knew this was going to take time.

Our neighborhood pool provided the kids and I the opportunity most summer days to have a change of scenery and expend
some excess energy, primarily for the kids, since I didn't have that
issue. In previous summers, I had continued to work full-time and
didn't know most of the folks who were active members of the
pool community including its administration and the very active
swim team. This summer, I stepped into a vibrant community of
much needed positivity and support that builds up kids and adults
through time together at the pool.

One of the first people I met was Jen. She was a warm,
engaging mom of four, and best friend of the sister of one of
Vince's high school mates. I knew this connection but did not
remember if Jen and I had previously met. Jen's kids were avid

swimmers, and her family was active in the pool community. This was part of her world into which I had entered, and she instantly welcomed me and the kids. Jen has a big heart and a calming way that allows you to trust her easily. She always greeted me with a genuine smile, probably having no idea, at least at first, the boost she was providing to each of my long days.

Jen is a great listener and an empathetic soul. She lost her own mother at the age of 10 but embodies the spirit and love of her amazing mom whom she has so eloquently described and shared with those who know her. Jen makes people feel seen and loved. Her impact in this period of my life is somewhat outsized when compared to the length of time we had known each other and what, if anything, I was able to offer in return. My gratitude for her compassion is eternal and I continue to be inspired by her gift of understanding. Thank you, Jen, for being you, for caring for us, and for continuing to shine your light. You are a reminder, to all of us, of the power of kindness.

CHAPTER 13

Becoming an American Family

From the moment we brought Jessi home and continuing for years, people would often ask about her. While I appreciated the concern, the mama in me always thought in the context of all three of my kids and I would always answer, "She's good. They're all good." We were all plugging away, one day at a time, together on this journey. Jessi rarely had a tantrum when one or both boys were home, and never when her dad was present. Vince once walked in when I had called him home from work to find me struggling on the floor to control Jessi. She immediately stopped fighting. Another day, I called Quinn, who was downstairs playing, up to Jessi's room during a tantrum so that he could see I wasn't hurting her. It must have sounded like I was throwing her around the room. When he came to the doorway, he saw that I was sitting across the small room from Jessi, as she fought her way through this episode. It was important to me that the boys and Vince see I was not treating Jessi differently than the boys and had not resorted to physical discipline.

As Boston and Quinn experienced glimpses of what I was facing each day, they became somewhat defensive of me. Vince and I reminded them to stay supportive of Jessi, not to be cold to her in trying to take my side. We reminded them that we were all on the same team and that she needed their unconditional love and support. I told them that I would be okay, and we would all get through this. To their credit, at nine and 11 years old, they did it. They accepted and grew to love their sister and continued to be the glue of the family. They never asked Vince and I why we adopted or complained about having a new little sister. As the tantrums subsided, the family dynamics became more and more normal. In these early days, Jessi had not yet become the classic 'annoying little sister' and the boys worked hard to help her learn and to have fun together. They said a friend or two had asked about Jessi, since they had never previously seen her. The boys explained she was their new sister and that we had recently adopted her.

The three kids share sibling bonds in all directions. Each of the boys has a unique relationship with Jessi, built upon the strengths and gifts they possess. They have developed deep, loving relationships colored with the standard sibling rivalries and jokes. They each communicate differently and feel proud of each other for various achievements and successes. They have some similar interests and many differences. Together, they serve as testimony of the human capacity to love and accept others in meeting the deep need for a sense of connection and belonging.

As mentioned, cocooning is recommended when you bring home an adoptive child. There is great potential for overwhelm on top of confusion while the entire family is working on forming connections and attachment. Our family's life centered, then as at the time of publication, heavily on school and athletics. From the time Jessi arrived, she was going along to sports games which were helpful in lowering stress for all of us. Sports allowed us to be outside, avoided Jessi and I being home alone, and provided Jessi a chance to see other kids and families interacting. Having seen firsthand in Thailand that Jessi was very much aware of the voyeuristic nature of people when she was with her new family, we were mindful to avoid similar scenarios as best we could. We did not initially have visitors in our home and did not immediately visit others, as our close family members did not live nearby.

As we celebrated Mother's Day and Father's Day, I realized how many more holidays and birthdays would come and go before finally getting to Jessi's birthday. We decided to have a five and a half birthday celebration, which was also her first birthday celebration ever. I knew she would have no sense of time to notice when her actual birthday rolled around that it had only been six months. And what kid would complain about an extra birthday party? We invited two other little girls Jessi had met at the pool including Jen's daughter. We also included my cousin, who is like a brother to me, and his two daughters who are close in age and relationship to the boys. We had balloons, cake, and presents. The four older kids did a great job entertaining the girls in the backyard including rides down the hill in a Thai pushcart we had brought back with us. It was a happy day for Jessi and, symbolically, it made up for the several prior birthdays she had not had the opportunity to celebrate.

I was torn between wanting to share with family and wanting to shelter our daughter. Because I was functioning daily through a high level of anxiety, the idea of being around anyone who might add to that was almost more than I could take. At this time, that meant basically everyone outside of our immediate family. Not long after Jessi came home, my father-in-law was set to receive an award honoring his life of impact in service to students during his dedicated career as an educator and administrator. Vince has always been very close to his father and I, too, developed a close relationship with this tower of a man. PopPop means the world to us all and has often been a bridge of understanding and patience within the family as his sons became adults and made their own families. We would not have missed this celebration for anything, and we were also nervous about how things would go with Jessi. Ultimately, it was a beautiful day honoring a great man, along with some other lifetime educators, and took our focus away from the intensity of adoption transition for a few hours.

For the July 4th holiday, we planned to visit the Eastern Shore of Maryland, to meet up with my mom, my brothers, and their families. At some point during the trip, Jessi and I found ourselves alone at the house and something triggered a tantrum. We were just over two months into the transition and tantrums were still very much a part of life. I remained anxious but was determined to keep moving forward because living in a bubble for too long was not good for anyone. My family was empathetic and supportive while meeting Jessi. I'm sure they were curious, but I didn't feel judged by them. Beyond the tantrum, most of what I recall is time together at the beach and at the house, playing outside, and being with my sisters-in-law. The visit provided temporary respite from being alone together as a newly formed family and began to introduce Jessi to more extended family.

We later visited the shore again to meet up with my parents-in-law while they were in town. My mother-in-law was bravely battling cancer and both she and PopPop were leaning on their faith and their love to get them through. We were all navigating significant challenges, unable to comprehend what each other was going through. Meanwhile, each of us was trudging through one day at a time without an instruction manual for the serious situations we faced. During this visit, Jessi did not have any tantrums. Thankfully, we later had opportunities to travel to Florida to visit them at home and make happy memories, after the tantrums had stopped.

Jessi had begun to grow attached to her daddy and was still forming a deeper connection, as with all of us. Once Jessi let down her guard with Vince, she seemed to notice the softness of other trusted male figures we had introduced including family members and friends and began to seek them out when they were around. It was like how she had interacted with female caregivers at The Babies Home where she was comfortable approaching someone she trusted and hugging their leg or leaning on them. Jessi didn't yet fully grasp the concept of family. She simply sought attention and security in whatever direction she could find it. Having had so little contact with men at The Babies Home, her behavior indicated she was rapidly growing more comfortable with male figures.

While I didn't personally have experience with a healthy father-daughter relationship, I knew that what I was seeing was not going to contribute to it for Vince or for Jessi. I felt protective of each of them and wanted their bond to have an opportunity to develop without the confusion of disparate attachments to other male figures so early on. I wanted, for them both, something I had personally never known but had witnessed in other families and between my father and my sister during sporadic visits. We gently dissuaded Jessi from too much physical contact with men besides Vince, preserving that space for the father-daughter connection to grow. Fortunately, this worked as she gravitated toward her dad and less so to every male figure she met. Over time, Jessi developed healthy relationships with loving family members and friends, regardless of gender.

In preparing for the school year, Jessi had been required to receive updated and some repeat vaccinations. As she sat in my lap, she had watched multiple needles be inserted into her arms without so much as a flinch or a sound. There was no visible or audible indication that she felt anything. I was astonished by her silence given the volume I had witnessed from her at home. It made me think about the concept of pain. Having been through a few months of outbursts, it seemed that, for Jessi, at least at this time, physical pain was tolerable, but emotional pain was almost unbearable. It was a fascinating and sad realization.

We had made it through summer, and it was time to begin school. I felt the usual mixed emotions of relief and anxiety. I was hopeful primarily because Marcia was Jessi's teacher and, in her, I knew we had an empathetic and committed partner. During the first week of kindergarten, Jessi went to the school nurse with a stomachache. When I received the call, I immediately thought it was a physical manifestation of stress or some other emotion Jessi had not released. I picked her up and took her to the pediatrician where they observed and assessed her without conclusion. They ruled out appendicitis based on the 'jump test.' It was explained to me that a person with an inflamed or ruptured appendix would not be able to jump on command due to the pain. When they asked Jessi to jump, she managed to get her heels off the floor, though her toes stayed in contact. It was enough that they thought it was beyond what she would be able to do if her appendix was in distress. I explained that having come from institutionalized care, she was predisposed to be compliant in response to someone in charge such as a doctor or nurse. We went home without a clear picture of what was going on.

Jessi returned to school a day or two later and the same thing occurred. At home, I observed her stools were loose, although not diarrhea. In considering appendicitis, this is a subtle but important distinction. Within about a day, she was walking hunched over, like a tiny, elderly person, slowly shuffling her feet. Having conducted my own online research, of course,

I was now convinced it was appendicitis. I took Jessi back to the pediatrician's office and was insistent that there was something serious going on. I asked how they could determine whether it was appendicitis. They did a blood test and found that her white blood cell count was elevated and explained I should take her to the emergency room.

The pediatrician's office called ahead, and the hospital was prepared for our arrival. Vince and the boys met us there. The emergency room staff conducted more tests including a CT scan and found Jessi's appendix had already ruptured. As the doctor relayed the news, he expressed amazement that Jessi was laying quietly in the hospital bed because any adult would be writhing in pain. He went on to say that, when Jessi got older, we should be sure to tell her the story and how strong she is. Unfortunately, Jessi's continued ability to withstand physical pain without reaction had enabled her to weather the storm in her body without clear outward indications. She still did not have the words to explain what she had been feeling and I had relied on observation, the internet, and my gut to help guide me. The doctor explained that Jessi needed to be moved to Children's National Hospital in Washington, D.C. and would be transported by ambulance, which I followed to Children's in my car.

It was late when we arrived at the hospital. Jessi was checked in and I was shown to her room. The staff attached her to monitors and started an IV to fight infection and control pain. Because Jessi's appendix had already ruptured, and coupled with her small size, surgery was too risky to be an option at this time. They needed to get the infection under control before her appendix could be safely surgically removed.

Over the next few weeks, Vince and I took turns being at the hospital with Jessi. She was never without one of us by her side while the other was home managing the house, getting the boys to and from school, and going into work periodically. There was a couch in the hospital room that was a better physical fit for me than for Vince, but he never complained. Sometimes, in the wee hours of the morning, I'd sit and watch Jessi sleeping. It was a quiet opportunity to simply be with her and love her without struggle for either of us. I felt as though I was getting back some of the time I'd missed when Jessi was a baby; that time when parents gaze in amazement at their child, falling in love. There had been so much turmoil in transition that I had never had that chance and I was grateful for this time. It was an unexpected silver lining. Whenever Jessi awoke, she saw Mom or Dad there, for her. Day by day, trust deepened, and the bond grew stronger in all directions.

Jessi's brothers visited her multiple times and family and friends sent flowers and gifts. We watched every children's show available and read books. Eventually, the infection was controlled enough to discharge Jessi, but we still had to wait about a month before surgery was possible. We took Jessi home with a colostomy bag to continue to drain harmful waste and she was not yet able to return to school. Jessi's classmates made her a poster and Marcia checked in regularly. She sent her a card and gift of a necklace that Jessi still has. While it was stressful to know Jessi was missing this early time in the school year to connect with her classmates, the blessing we received was the unexpected connection with family through quiet moments provided by an additional challenge.

One month later, Jessi's appendix was successfully removed. She returned to school. There were no more tantrums. We had turned a corner.

With things having settled, a lot, we began to consider the possibility of enrolling Jessi in some extracurricular activities. Before Jessi came home, we had no preconceived notions about her talents or what interests she might develop. We made no assumptions and had no specific expectations. Of course, it's easy to go with what you know, which for me was dance and field hockey. However, opting to pursue those activities with Jessi had been inspired by comments from The Babies Home and our own observations of Jessi. One day playing at home, Jessi picked up a plastic racket, started swatting a ball back and forth around the floor, and moving around the room. My heart leapt at this sight. Shortly after, we gave Jessi the opportunity to try field hockey, a sport I had played and coached for decades. She has since tried multiple other sports as well. Sports certainly aren't the only way to teach life and leadership lessons to kids, but they're one of the best.

Dance was a bit more of a strategic choice for teaching not only self-leadership but establishing the brain and body connection. We knew Jessi had participated in Thai dance at The Babies Home, and we saw this as a natural extension with multiple benefits for her overall development. I had been a dancer at various times earlier in life and knew, firsthand, the body control and mental focus that could be gained through dance. While Jessi had some athletic ability, she lacked strength and command of her body. An observable example that occurred repeatedly was the way she would flap her arms as she descended stairs in the house. She had very little muscle development in her legs, and none in her core, to help her balance. While I had personally never studied ballet, some of my fellow hip-hop dancers were technically trained prior to pursuing other styles. It sometimes seemed difficult for some of the ballet dancers to loosen up for styles such as hip hop, but their complete control of every movement was impressive.

I began to research local dance schools, close to home. We attended a beginner ballet class to observe. The class we attended lacked diversity and the overall branding of the studio seemed to promote a pre-company track from the beginning. It was an established and successful program but didn't feel right for Jessi. I found another school with a completely different vibe – Princess Mhoon Dance Institute (PMDI). Equally professional with an accomplished director whose name was Princess Mhoon. I was so intrigued. The website and branding showed a diverse and inclusive student body and made clear their philosophy that dance is for everyone and every body. I enrolled Jessi in a summer dance camp at PMDI and, later, beginner ballet. In this space, most of the ballerinas looked more like Jessi than me. The beauty of a studio full of mostly brown ballerinas, so young that this was their normal, was simply breathtaking and inspiring. Just one year prior, Misty Copeland had become the first African American female principal dancer with the American Ballet Theater. The PMDI experience, under the direction of the force that is Princess Mhoon, and her wonderful team, was a formative one for Jessi. While she didn't fall in love with ballet, she developed additional patience, focus, and discipline of body movement. Maybe one day she'll return to a dance studio to pursue a style of her own choosing.

We are fortunate to live in an area with a diverse population including food and religious options for many cultures and countries of origin. Wat Thai DC is one of the largest Thai temples in the Washington, D.C. area and is located just six miles from our house. We had previously visited Wat Thai DC with my Thai language teacher, so I knew to explore it for cultural education and celebrations. During pre-pandemic times, Wat Thai DC offered weekend training throughout the year and a summer school program. However, when Jessi first came home, we wanted her to have an opportunity to begin to learn American culture and to bond with her family. We were somewhat concerned that being around so many Thai people would make her homesick in a way that wasn't helpful for her.

In October 2016, Thai King Bhumibol Adulyadej passed away. He was the third-longest reigning monarch in global history, having held his role for over 70 years, and having been served by 30 prime ministers. It was an event of significant magnitude and loss for Thailand and Thai people the world over. While on vacations in Thailand, I had grown accustomed to seeing King Bhumibol's photo everywhere, literally everywhere, I went in Thailand. Before all events, from watching movies to sporting events, the King's anthem was played out of respect. Because his health had gone up and down in his older years, whenever I traveled to Thailand, the Thai people seemed always prepared to recognize a long period of mourning, should the unthinkable occur. Even though it occurred after I had come back to the U.S., I felt deep sadness for Thailand and its people who were experiencing grief and loss. I took Jessi to the temple to pay our respects.

By the following summer, we were anxious to get Jessi reconnected with her roots and have her around Thai speakers and Thai people. She was able to attend a full running of the summer school program and quickly became reaccustomed to being around monks and Thai people, mostly Thai-Americans fluent in both Thai and English. Through this program, Jessi began to learn to play the Thai instrument called the 'khim' (keem). It seemed most of the kids who attended Wat Thai DC had one or two Thai parents. It never seemed to phase Jessi and, at her younger age at the time, she may not have noticed, certainly not to the level I did. This said, she noticed what the other kids brought for lunch, such as rice and noodles, versus the sandwich I often sent. I picked up on it one evening when she asked if she could have some leftovers from dinner, which included rice, for lunch the next day. I tried to incorporate more of the foods that were both her favorites and allowed her to fit in with her Thai-American peers.

This is an element of life and identity that is truly Jessi's to own and of which to be proud. She was comfortable at the

wat whereas her brothers are less so. It's difficult when the cere-
monies go on for extended periods and you can't understand a
word being spoken. I once ended up sitting in on a funeral for
someone I didn't know, thinking I had joined a standard service.
Fortunately, there were other 'farangs' in the room and no one
thought it strange to see me there, as I realized midway through
that I had joined the wrong gathering.

We have always been welcomed at Wat Thai DC, and I
appreciated the standard Thai hospitality, particularly in those
first years. It is hard sometimes to get updated information since
I can't read Thai and I have relied on a kind mom to assist me in
making sure I understood where Jessi needed to be and when.
While the weekend times throughout the year often conflicted
with athletic events, Jessi attended Thai dance regularly until the
COVID-19 pandemic.

During our six-month probationary period, we had home
visits by an American social worker every two months, who then
sent the results to Thailand. Following the three visits, which
was ultimately probably longer than six months, we again waited
for the Thai Board approval for our family to move forward with
finalization of the adoption in the U.S. Jessi had entered the U.S.
on a Thai passport, with a U.S. immigrant visa, and was later
issued a green card. Some other countries' adoption finalization
processes are different in that the child becomes a citizen when
they arrive in the U.S. Once we received the final approval to

finalize from the Thai government, we then had to file through the U.S. court system.

Many families probably hire an adoption lawyer to help with this part and I'm sure there is something to be said for the convenience and professionalism they provide. By now, however, I no longer wanted to spend money on process. I took some time and researched various options including adoption lawyers and how to petition the court on your own behalf. After doing some digging, I eventually found a website on which a lawyer had laid out the steps for drafting your own petition and I got to work. The petition includes a description of the circumstances that led to the adoption. It was somewhat surreal to translate what was a very emotional story and journey into a purely legal and clinical context for presentation to the court. I drafted the language and requested the assistance of a close friend, who is an attorney, in formatting the petition to meet court standards. It worked. The court approved the petition, and we were required to appear before the court to finalize the adoption, 18 months after bringing Jessi home.

Even after adoption finalization, when U.S. citizenship is technically granted, the newly minted U.S. citizen has no proof of U.S. citizenship. It is an important final step to file an Application for Certificate of Citizenship (N-600) with U.S. Citizen and Immigration Services. This documentation is what will allow an adopted child to get a U.S. passport and meet formal requests for U.S. citizenship status throughout their life. Once more, the family must provide copies of the multitude of documents compiled many times throughout the adoption process. Fortunately, USCIS offers electronic submission, although the child and parent must also appear in person for biometrics and then wait again. The application cost $1,170 U.S. dollars, when we applied, and we were prepared for many more months of waiting to hear back. In our case, the five months of waiting seemed short compared to the many years leading up to this point. Jessi was granted her Certificate of Citizenship just before publication; finally able to call the U.S. home and one step closer to being able to visit her birth country. Our journey continues.

Everyone in the sphere of adoption learns something and gains perspective. In this way, adoption is normalized in society, but the view from the inside will always be different than the fishbowl optic. It is my hope that our family's experience enlightens additional elements of this monumental act of faith to help people support others in the process and transition. And maybe, a family somewhere will be inspired, encouraged, and moved to heed the call in their heart, and go into it with eyes wide open. They and a child will be forever changed because of it. Just as we have been.

Afterword

Adoption is a lifelong journey we're on together as a family. Two of us chose adoption. Three of us did not. And yet, all three kids have chosen love and family. I sometimes read or hear stories about other adoptive families in which the attachment issues are a significant challenge. We have been so blessed that Jessi became deeply attached to each of us and we to her. She is a deep feeling, strong, intelligent person. If you met her, you would have no idea of the struggles we faced in the early days and all that she has gone through in becoming the tween she is at the time of this writing. That's a wonderful thing.

Jessi doesn't view the fact that she is adopted as a free pass in terms of accountability and responsibility for herself. There is no need to lower expectations for her. She continues to demonstrate she can rise to the challenges that come her way. Jessi is unashamed to say she is adopted and recognizes the uniqueness of her background compared to many of her peers. It is another element of her identity that we seek to develop through opportunities for relationships with other kids who understand. And she will continue to explore her origins throughout her life.

One of Jessi's most special bonds developed in the years since finalization is with my mother, whom the kids call 'Bella.' When the boys were little, they couldn't say 'Grandmom', and they already called Vince's mom 'MomMom'. I suggested 'abuela,' the Spanish word for grandmother, and 'Bella' it became. Jessi and Bella love and accept each other as they are. I joke that they sometimes sound like two old women friends or two giggly girlfriends. This bond took time, just as they all did. My mom was unsure how the relationship would develop. She had raised three children and had become a grandmother several years prior. However, meeting your new granddaughter as a fully formed person who speaks another language can be intimidating, even for an adult. My mom was helpful for me in discerning which behavioral issues were related to gender, age, adoption, or some combination thereof, and whether they mattered enough to address. Bella ensures traditions live on and she has been attentive to helping fill in those gaps for Jessi from classic Christmas cartoons to old school strawberry shortcake in a dessert cake cup. We are so grateful that Jessi is experiencing one of life's most special bonds in a way some biological kids may not even have the opportunity to.

One of our family traditions honoring Jessi's Thai culture is to include a fresh pineapple in holiday meals, and often in between. It is both Jessi's favorite fruit and my favorite Thai word (saparot, pronounced 'sa-pa-lote'). Jessi loves going to H-Mart to get authentic Asian and Thai ingredients for cooking and try interesting Asian snacks. We alternate between potatoes for Quinn and rice for Jessi; Vince and Boston will eat anything. Pineapple will always taste sweeter in Thailand, and we look forward to taking Jessi back to reconnect to her roots. For now, pineapple holds the promise of Jessi's forever family and our commitment to honoring all that she is and supporting all that she will become. Sawatdi kha!

Key Concepts to Consider and Explore

(For discussion or as journal prompts.)

1. Adoption is a complex, lifelong process, and affects everyone in the family. What is something in this story that surprised you about adoption?

2. There is no positive scenario which causes a child to lose one or both parents. What is another scenario that involves both love and loss?

3. If you meet someone adopted, be empathetic about the personal nature of their story. Do you know anyone that you are aware is adopted? Do they ever share anything about it?

4. Everyone you meet carries a story with them. Be kind. It's okay to be curious but don't ask intrusive questions. Can you think of a time you might have asked a question that was too personal? How could you have approached it differently?

5. Teach children to respect boundaries, at home, and with other people. Do so yourself. In what ways do you set boundaries in your life? How can you respect them with others?

6. If you have a calling, answer it. You have a purpose. Have you ever felt you have a calling? Do you feel you know your purpose?

7. When you understand your why, you will always figure out how. Can you think of a time that your reason for doing something helped you see it through even when it was hard?

8. Control what you can control. Never let *you* be what's holding you back. Can you think of an area or situation in your life where you focused on things outside of your control?

9. Difficult doesn't mean impossible. Take one step at a time. What is a big goal you would like to achieve? What is one step you can take now to move towards it?

10. Commitment and determination will allow you to do hard things. What is an example in your life where this has proven true for you? How can you apply it in your life now?

11. Open your mind to allow your thinking to evolve and make space to examine your beliefs. What is one belief you have held all your life? Have you ever considered other ways of looking at the issue or other perspectives?

12. Opportunity is everything. Stand in the gap for others. Can you think of an example in which someone has provided you an opportunity that made a difference in your life?

13. Do what you can when you can. Helpers need help sometimes too. Ask for and accept it. When was a time you needed help? Did you ask for it?

14. The human capacity to love and connect with others extends beyond blood. Who is someone you love deeply who is not your blood relative?

15. Love is a universal language. It can be spoken with smiles and hugs. Have you ever felt a connection with someone without speaking to each other?

16. Leadership begins with self. Always start there and lead from where you are. Can you think of a time you led in a situation without being in a leadership position?

17. Identity is multi-faceted. Explore and honor all parts of yourself. List as many parts of your identity as you can. Are there any parts you would like to change *or* more fully honor? What is one thing you can do starting now to accomplish that?

18. Strive for connection with who you are, the unique essence with which you were born. What parts of you have never changed from the time you were very young?

19. Every person is born worthy of love and belonging. In what scenario(s) and with which people do you feel the most comfortable and connected?

20. You are enough. Speak to yourself the way you would speak to a friend. Say to yourself "I am enough" and believe it.